Popular Mechanics FOR KIDS

Make Cool Gadgets for Your Room

Amy Pinchuk

Illustrated by Teco Rodrigues

HarperTrophy®
An Imprint of HarperCollinsPublishers

First published in Canada by Greey de Pencier Books Inc. in 2001
First United States edition published by HarperCollins Children's Books, a
division of HarperCollins*Publishers,* in 2001

"Popular Mechanics for Kids" is a trademark of Hearst Communications, Inc.

Make Cool Gadgets for Your Room
Text © 2001 by Amy Pinchuk
Illustrations © 2001 by Teco Rodrigues

Also available: *Make Amazing Toy and Game Gadgets*

Dedication
To Mark and our children, Matthew, Rachel, Paul, and Daniel, who have engi-
neered a great family.

Acknowledgments
Thank you, Sheba, for your inspiration and guidance in writing this book,
Keltie for editing it, and Word & Image for making it look great. Thanks also
to the following people for putting up with me during this time, answering
questions, and providing ideas: Mark, Matthew, Rachel, Paul, Daniel, David,
Josh, Lenny, Dad, Mom, R. Pardoe, J. Konrad, R. Paknys, M. Marks, and the
Vineberg family. Finally, I would like to thank all of those "experts" out there
who replied to my e-mail queries on many of the subjects contained in this
book.

#JNF 3-2-02

Library of Congress catalog number: 00-108170
ISBN 0-688-17798-0
ISBN 0-688-17727-1 (pbk.)

Design & Art Direction: Word & Image Design Studio
Illustrations: Teco Rodrigues
Photography: Ray Boudreau

Printed in Hong Kong

1   2   3   4   5   6   7   8   9   10

Contents

Build Cool Gadgets, Now!

Put your building cap on, roll up your sleeves, and make some truly amazing gadgets to jazz up your room. All of these nifty gadgets are made of buzzers that buzz, parts that move, and lights that flash. So they're fun to build and play around with. What's more, they'll make your room the coolest place to hang out in the neighborhood.

Flashy Key Chain

You won't want to leave your room without it. Made out of a bottle top, you can push and pull its flashing light on and off. Clip it on your belt loop or backpack and flash on!

Secret Code Machine

Build the Secret Code Machine to encode and decode secret messages for your eyes and your friends' eyes only.

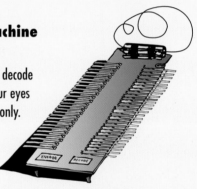

See It, Hear It Doorbell

Wire up the See It, Hear It Doorbell and no one will ever barge into your room unannounced again. It lights up when it rings!

Quiz Game

Host your own game show with this electronic Quiz Game. Touch the questions and watch the board light up with the right answers.

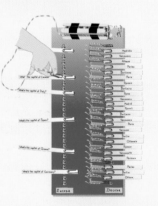

Bouncy Animal

Power up your favorite hand puppet or stuffed animal with an electric motor and watch it spin around your room.

Alarm in a Box

Bzzzzt! Wire up a box with an alarm that goes on whenever anyone opens the box unless it's disarmed with a secret code that only you know!

Start by choosing a cool gadget that you want to make. Then carefully read through all the step-by-step instructions. This will give you an idea of what you're going to do and what to expect along the way.

■ Your personal guide leads you through the tough parts and tells you what to watch out for as you build.

■ Step-by-step pictures and instructions show you how to make each gadget.

■ **Zoom In on the Mechanics** gives you the inside scoop on how each gadget works.

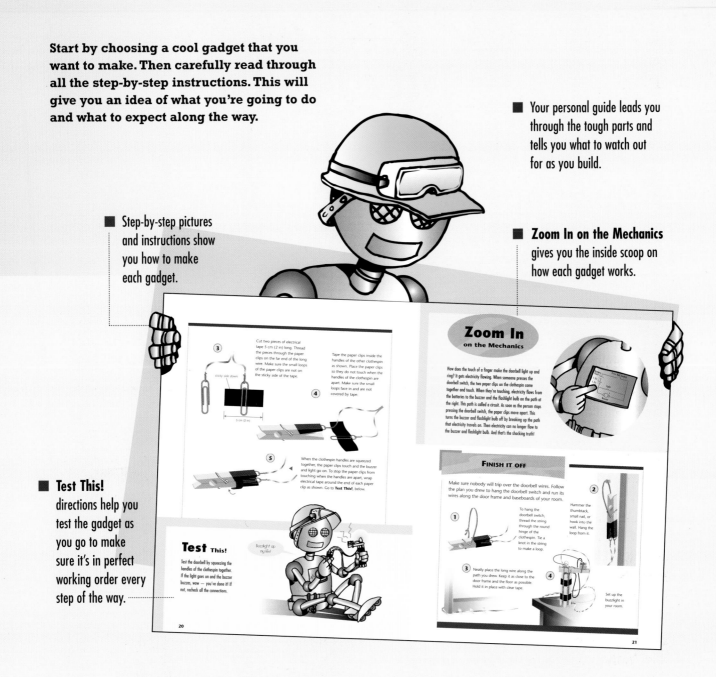

■ **Test This!** directions help you test the gadget as you go to make sure it's in perfect working order every step of the way.

Once you've chosen a project, take a good look at **Tools & Stuff You Need** on the first page of the activity. Chances are you'll be able to find most of these things around your home, and you'll have a few things to buy from local hardware or electronic stores.

Gather up what you've got at home, make a shopping list, and buy what you need. If you can't find exactly what's called for, try to find something similar. For example, use Bristol™ board instead of index cards. But when it comes to electrical stuff like wires, batteries, and electrical tape, play it safe by using exactly what's listed. Check out **The "What's That?" Glossary** on page 62 and **How-to Tips** on page 59 to find out more about what things are and how to use them. Get going and have fun!

Put Safety First

When it comes to building mechanical gadgets and working with electrical gizmos, pros always put safety first. The pros check and test what they're building every step of the way. They also make sure their finished product is neat and tidy so it is safe to use.

All of the gadgets described in this book are perfectly safe to make. The step-by-step instructions for building them are based on the methods of the pros. When extra safety caution is needed for certain steps, the instructions tell you to wear safety goggles or to get an adult to help. The activities in this book are for kids at least nine years old. Keep all materials out of the reach of younger children.

Here are a few golden rules to help you play it safe:

• Handle all tools with care.

• All the gadgets use regular batteries. Use only the batteries listed. NEVER try to make or use any of the gadgets with other power sources like the plug-in outlets in your home or larger batteries. That's a double D: dumb and dangerous!

• Read over and follow any directions that come with the stuff you're working with such as glue, buzzers, batteries, and resistors.

• Take special care when you're working with glue. When using drills, X-Acto knives, and other cutting tools, always work with an adult. Never drill or cut toward your body or your hands. Make sure you don't damage any furniture or surfaces around you.

• If you're not sure about something, ask an adult for help.

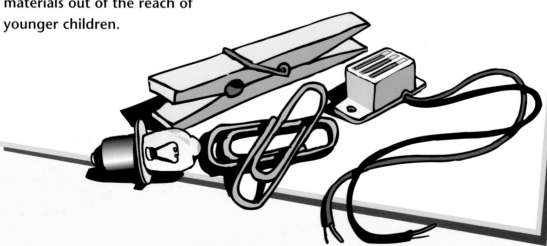

Flashy Key Chain

You won't find this key chain in any store. It's a flashy one-of-a-kind that will draw attention to your keys so you won't forget them. Push it and a flashing light comes on—blink, blink. Pull it and the light goes off. Put in your pocket. Or hang it on your backpack and flash on!

Tools & Stuff You Need

- safety goggles
- drill, scissors, needle-nose pliers or tweezers
- manicure scissors or sharp pointy knife
- 3-volt battery the size of a coin
- 1.5- to 3-volt blinking LED with leads about 3 cm ($1\frac{1}{4}$ in) long
- key ring
- push-pull top from a water or dishwashing liquid bottle
- small plastic straw about 0.5 cm ($\frac{1}{4}$ in) wide, toothpicks
- pencil, black marker, ruler, masking tape
- 5-minute epoxy glue

RIG THE BOTTLE TOP

Check out your bottle top. Does it slide up and down about 3 mm ($\frac{1}{8}$ in)? If not, use another one.

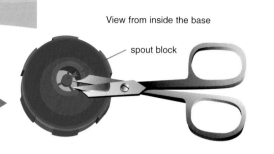

View from inside the base

spout block

1

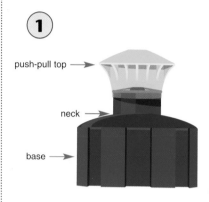

push-pull top →

neck →

base →

With an adult, use the manicure scissors or the knife to cut off the spout block. Looking from inside the base, most spout blocks are held in place by plastic bits. Cut the bits as close to the top's wall as you can. Remove the bits and the spout block. Go to **Test This!**

2

Wear safety goggles for this step. Have an adult help you drill a small hole for the key ring where shown.

Test This!

After you cut off the spout block, push and pull the top to make sure it still slides well. If it doesn't, check if one of the plastic bits got stuck in the top. If it still doesn't slide well, use a different bottle top.

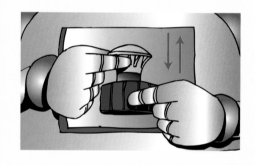

That Blinking TV

Would you believe the picture on your TV blinks 30 times a second and you've never noticed? The light on the Flashy Key Chain blinks about two times a second and you can see the blinking. But if a light or picture blinks more than 10 times a second, you don't see the blinking because your brain fills in the blank spots. Your brain makes you think the light or picture is still on even though it's off. No kidding! Although the picture on your TV looks like it's on all the time, it's actually being redrawn 30 times a second!

INSTALL THE FLASHING LIGHT

Get set to turn an ordinary bottle top into something flashy!

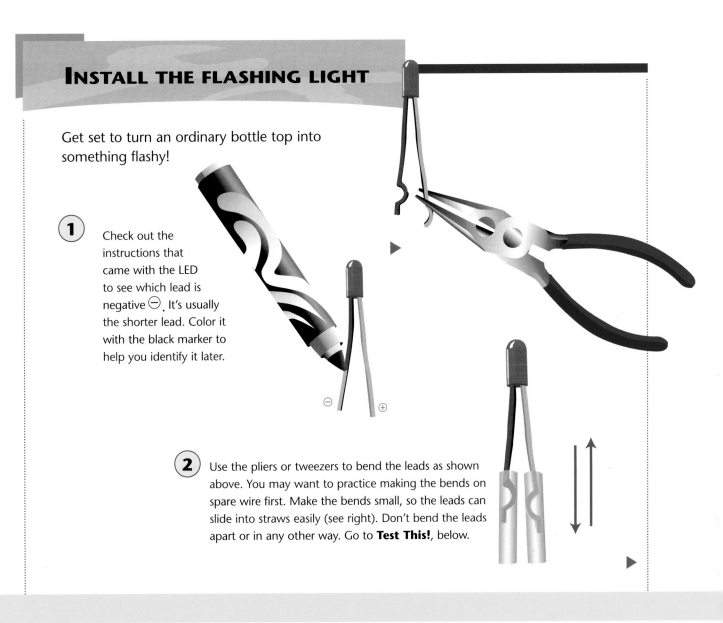

1 Check out the instructions that came with the LED to see which lead is negative ⊖. It's usually the shorter lead. Color it with the black marker to help you identify it later.

2 Use the pliers or tweezers to bend the leads as shown above. You may want to practice making the bends on spare wire first. Make the bends small, so the leads can slide into straws easily (see right). Don't bend the leads apart or in any other way. Go to **Test This!**, below.

Test This!

Test the LED before you install it. Check out the instructions with the battery to find the battery's ⊖ terminal. Place the battery between the LED leads so the ⊖ lead touches the ⊖ terminal of the battery and the positive ⊕ lead touches the ⊕ terminal. Does the LED light blink? If so, everything is A-OK! If not, check that the correct leads and battery terminals are touching. Also, check if it's too bright in the room to see the blinking by doing this test in a darker spot. If it still doesn't work, the LED or the battery needs to be replaced.

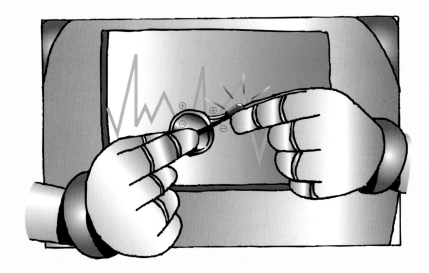

③ 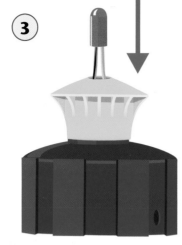 Carefully insert the leads in the top hole of the bottle top. Push the light bulb down, so it sits just above the hole.

⑤

④  Turn the light bulb so the ⊕ lead faces the key ring hole.

Glue the light bulb on the bottle top. Use a toothpick to apply the epoxy glue around the bottom of the light bulb. See epoxy glue tips, page 60. Don't get the glue all over the LED leads. Let it dry for 20 minutes.

Frog Power

Believe it or not, a dead frog was the world's first battery! In 1786, a scientist named Galvani noticed that when two different metals touched a dead frog's leg, the leg jumped. (Bet Galvani jumped, too!) Then another scientist named Volta discovered that it wasn't the frog's leg that caused the shocking result. It was a chemical reaction in which electricity flowed between the metals used to make the "frog sandwich." Since then, batteries have been made with chemicals instead of frogs. Galvani had the galvanometer, a device that measures electric current, named after him, and Volta had volts, which measure the strength of batteries, named after him. But the poor litttle frog never had anything named after him. Go figure!

ADD BATTERY POWER

Make the LED flash with a battery that looks like a nickel.

The ⊕ side of this battery is marked, the ⊖ side is blank.

clean zone

5mm (¼ in)

1

5mm (¼ in)

Pull up the top. Measure the length of the bottle top's neck by inserting the straw into the top as far as it will go and marking where it comes out. Cut two straw pieces 5 mm (¼ in) longer than the neck.

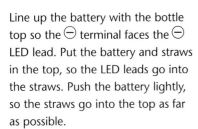

2

Glue one straw piece on each side of the battery as shown. Put tape on the battery's "clean zone" to keep it free of glue. Don't get glue around the openings of the straws. Use a toothpick to apply epoxy glue along the top 5 mm (¼ in) of the straws. Let it dry for 20 minutes. Then remove the tape.

3

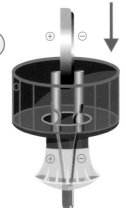

⊕   ⊖

⊕   ⊖

Line up the battery with the bottle top so the ⊖ terminal faces the ⊖ LED lead. Put the battery and straws in the top, so the LED leads go into the straws. Push the battery lightly, so the straws go into the top as far as possible.

Push down the top. Check if the bends in the leads come out of the straws to touch the battery. If not, remove the battery and straws. Then trim the free ends of the straws with the scissors. Go to **Test This!**, below.

4

▶

Test This!

- After you've done step 4 above, test out the LED and battery set up. Push the top down. Does the light blink? If so, it's working! Skip the next step.
- If not, check that the bends on the LED leads come out of the straws to touch the battery. Make sure the bends can make good contact with the battery and no glue is in the way. Also, check the position of the battery. The ⊖ terminal should touch the ⊖ lead and the ⊕ terminal should touch the ⊕ lead.
- OK, the push mechanism is working. Now test the pull. Pull the top up. Does the light stop blinking? If so, skip the next step.

- If not, check that the leads go back into the straws and no longer touch the battery. If the leads don't go in all the way, pull out the battery and straws a bit until you find the right position as shown above.
- Try the push and pull mechanisms a few more times to make sure they're working well. Go to step 5, next page.

5 Once the push and pull mechanisms work well and the straws are the right length and in the right place, glue the straws to the top. Don't get the epoxy glue on the battery or LED leads. Use a toothpick to put it on the top's neck and straws.

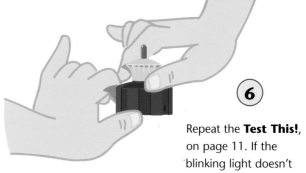

6 Repeat the **Test This!**, on page 11. If the blinking light doesn't work now, you probably got glue on one of the LED leads or the battery's clean zone. Scrape it off with a scissors' blade. Also, check that you removed the tape from the battery.

ADD THE KEY RING

A key ring makes your Flashy Key Chain complete.

1 Insert the key ring through the hole you drilled. Have fun with it!

WARNING!
If you twist or turn the bottle top, it may stop working. To fix it, look inside the bottom of the top and slowly untwist the cap until the LED leads straighten up inside the straws.

Zoom In
on the Mechanics

Just how does your Flashy Key Chain work? If you're thinking it all comes down to the push-pull mechanism of the bottle top, you're right! When you push the top down, the LED leads move out of the straws and touch the battery. (The bend you put in the leads helps them touch the battery. You also placed the battery where they can make good contact with it.) Then power from the battery flows into the LED to make it flash. When you pull the top up, the leads move into the straws, which stop them from touching the battery. Then power stops flowing and the LED stops flashing. That's it in a flash!

See It, Hear It Doorbell

Flash! Buzz! Flash! Buzz! Hey, it looks and sounds like you've got company. The See It, Hear It Doorbell lights up when it rings just to make doubly sure you know there's a visitor at the door. Make it for your bedroom and "buzzlight" up your life.

Tools & Stuff You Need

- hammer, wire cutters, wire stripper, scissors, tape measure
- 10 Popsicle sticks, 2 clothespins, 5 large elastic bands, clear tape
- small nail or hook or thumbtack
- 6 unpainted metal paper clips
- 2 C batteries
- 7.6 m (25 ft) of speaker wire*

- 15 cm (6 in) of string or ribbon
- 3-volt DC mini buzzer "normally off"
- 3-volt DC mini flashlight bulb
- electrical tape
- paper, pencil

* See page 63 for notes

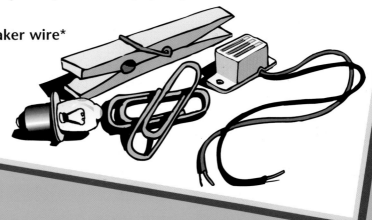

MAKE A BATTERY PACK

Build a battery pack out of Popsicle sticks, elastics, and tape. It'll keep the batteries touching each other so that power can flow to the doorbell.

Got all this stuff you need?

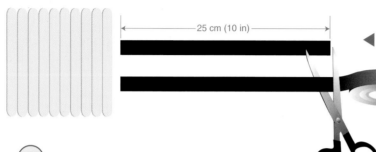

1 Place 10 Popsicle sticks beside each other as shown. Use the scissors to cut two pieces of electrical tape about 25 cm (10 in) long.

25 cm (10 in)

2

4 cm (1½ in)

2.5 cm (1 in)

▲ Stick the tape on the Popsicle sticks, so 4 cm (1½ in) of tape is left on one side.

sticky side up

3 Turn over the Popsicle sticks, so the tape is sticky side up. Take out every second Popsicle stick.

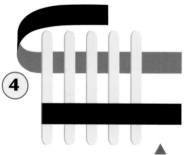

4

▲ Put the long end of the tape over the Popsicle sticks. Press it down so it sticks to itself between the Popsicle sticks.

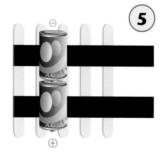

5 On a gap between two Popsicle sticks, stack the batteries as shown. Make sure the negative ⊖ terminal of one battery touches the positive ⊕ terminal of the other. Then line up the other ⊖ terminal with the top of the sticks.

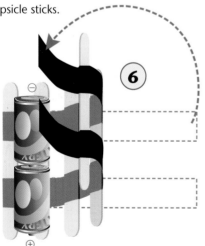

6 ◀ Wrap the Popsicle sticks tightly around the batteries as shown. Close up the battery pack with the tape.

7 Put two elastic bands around the battery pack as shown to keep the batteries in contact with each other.

BUILD THE BUZZER CIRCUIT

Get set to connect and test the doorbell buzzer.

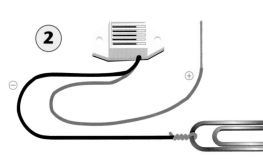

1

Use the wire stripper to strip 2.5 cm (1 in) of insulation from the end of each buzzer wire. If the buzzer doesn't have wires, split some speaker wire into two wires and strip all the ends. Connect one end of one wire to the ⊕ terminal of the buzzer and one end of the other to the ⊖ terminal. See wire stripping and connecting tips, page 60.

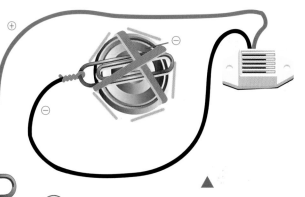

2

On some buzzers, the black wire is ⊖ and the red is ⊕. Read the buzzer instructions to check. Loop and twist the ⊖ wire tightly around the big end of a paper clip.

3 Slip the paper clip under the elastics on the ⊖ terminal of the battery pack. Make sure it is touching the terminal. Go to **Test This!**, next page.

Best Before 500 BC

Can you imagine batteries with expiration dates of 500 BC?! Archeologists have dug up some batteries that may be this old near Baghdad. These batteries are unlike any you've ever seen. They're made out of big clay vases. Inside the vases, there's a hollow copper tube with an iron rod in the middle. Archeologists think the vases were filled with vinegar or lemon juice to make a chemical reaction, which caused electricity to flow from the copper to the iron. That's a lot like batteries work today. But what were they used for back then? No one knows. Archeologists have a few guesses though, such as magic tricks and coating gold on jewelry!

Testing...bzzzt... testing!

Test This!

Test the buzzer and battery connections. Touch the end of the ⊕ buzzer wire to the ⊕ terminal of the battery pack. Does it buzz? If so, everything is working perfectly! If not, make sure that the stripped end of the ⊖ buzzer wire is well fastened to the paper clip and that the paper clip is pressing against the metal of the ⊖ battery terminal. Check that the batteries are touching each other. Also, check that the paper clip is metal and not painted. (Paint stops electricity from flowing through the paper clip.) If all these things check out and it still doesn't work, you may need to replace the buzzer or the batteries.

PLAN THE WIRE ROUTE

Take a building break. Draw a plan that shows where you will put the doorbell switch and the buzzlight.

1

Find a place for the doorbell switch near your bedroom door. You want it to be low enough for little people to reach, but high enough for big people to notice. Make sure the spot for the switch is close to the door frame. Then you'll be able to run wires, which will connect the switch to the buzzlight, along the seam between the door frame and the wall.

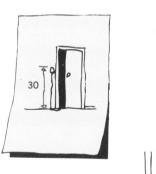

2

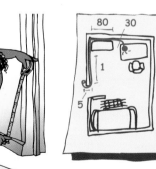

Choose a place to put the buzzlight where you'll notice it light up. On your plan, mark the path that the wires from the doorbell switch will take to reach the buzzlight. Make sure the wires go behind furniture — not in front.

Measure the path from the doorbell switch to the buzzlight to figure out how long a wire you need to connect them. Note the measurements on your plan.

MAKE THE LIGHT CIRCUIT

Team up a clothespin and a flashlight bulb to light up your life.

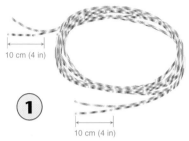

1

Measure a piece of speaker wire the length you determined in your plan. Before you cut the wire, run it along the path from the switch to the buzzlight to make sure it reaches all the way. Cut the wire with the wire cutters. Split 10 cm (4 in) of wire on both ends. See wire splitting tips, page 61.

Use the wire stripper to strip 2.5 cm (1 in) of insulation from all four wire ends.

2

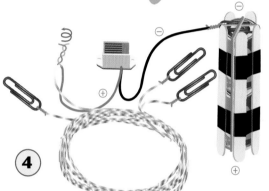

Loop and twist one end of the wire tightly around the big end of a paper clip. Repeat this for two of the remaining ends.

3

4

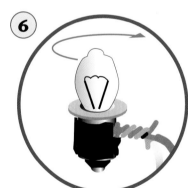

Twist together the free end of the wire and the ⊕ buzzer wire.

5

6

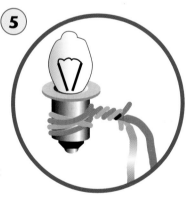

Wrap the twisted wires around the base of the flashlight bulb. Make sure the wires do not touch the bulb's bottom contact or stick out below it.

Use a small piece of electrical tape to hold the wires in place temporarily. Make sure the tape doesn't touch the glass or bottom contact of the bulb.

Clamp the wires onto the base of the bulb permanently by fitting the wire-wrapped base into the "hole" of the clothespin. Make sure the bottom contact of the bulb sticks out a bit below the clothespin, but that none of the stripped wires do. Go to **Test This!**, next page.

7

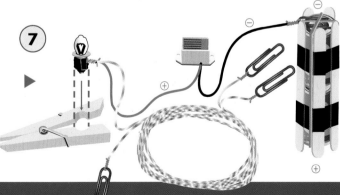

Test This!

Stop and test the connections you've just made. Hold the clothespin and touch the bottom contact of the flashlight bulb to the ⊖ terminal of the battery pack. (It's OK if the bottom contact touches the paper clip.) At the same time, touch the two paper clips on the far end of the long wire to the ⊕ terminal of the battery pack. Does the light go on? Does the buzzer buzz? If so, way to go! If not, recheck all the connections. If the light still doesn't go on but the buzzer buzzes, the bulb may be burnt out. Replace it.

GOT IT WORKING?

Use some elastic bands and tape to put your doorbell together.

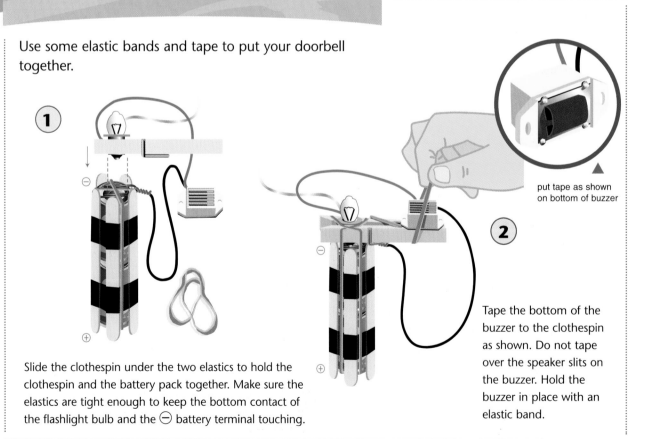

put tape as shown on bottom of buzzer

1 Slide the clothespin under the two elastics to hold the clothespin and the battery pack together. Make sure the elastics are tight enough to keep the bottom contact of the flashlight bulb and the ⊖ battery terminal touching.

2 Tape the bottom of the buzzer to the clothespin as shown. Do not tape over the speaker slits on the buzzer. Hold the buzzer in place with an elastic band.

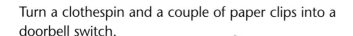

Turn a clothespin and a couple of paper clips into a doorbell switch.

Touch together the two paper clips that are on the far ends of the long wire. Hear the buzz and see the light? If not, check and secure all the connections.

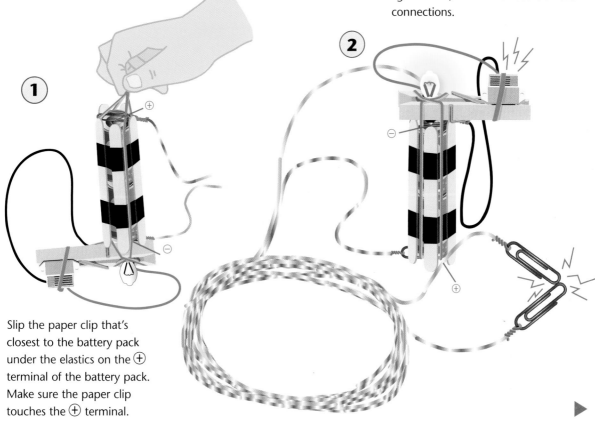

1 Slip the paper clip that's closest to the battery pack under the elastics on the ⊕ terminal of the battery pack. Make sure the paper clip touches the ⊕ terminal.

2

Watch that "Tongue" Glow

The glow of tungsten metal lights up your life almost everywhere you go. Inside most light bulbs, a small piece of tungsten wire sits on a metal stand. When electricity flows through the wire, the tungsten gets very hot — up to 2500°C (4500°F) — and glows. Tungsten breaks down as it glows. So light bulbs are filled with a special gas called argon to prevent the wire from rusting and burning out quickly. But eventually the wire breaks and then the bulb is "burnt out"!

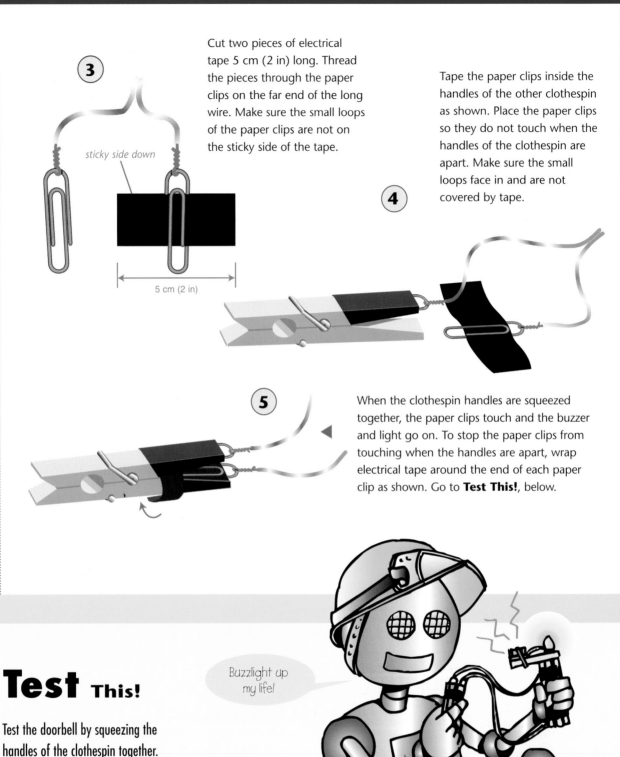

3

Cut two pieces of electrical tape 5 cm (2 in) long. Thread the pieces through the paper clips on the far end of the long wire. Make sure the small loops of the paper clips are not on the sticky side of the tape.

sticky side down

5 cm (2 in)

Tape the paper clips inside the handles of the other clothespin as shown. Place the paper clips so they do not touch when the handles of the clothespin are apart. Make sure the small loops face in and are not covered by tape.

4

5

When the clothespin handles are squeezed together, the paper clips touch and the buzzer and light go on. To stop the paper clips from touching when the handles are apart, wrap electrical tape around the end of each paper clip as shown. Go to **Test This!**, below.

Test **This!**

Test the doorbell by squeezing the handles of the clothespin together. If the light goes on and the buzzer buzzes, wow — you've done it! If not, recheck all the connections.

Buzzlight up my life!

Zoom In
on the Mechanics

How does the touch of a finger make the doorbell light up and ring? It gets electricity flowing. When someone presses the doorbell switch, the two paper clips on the clothespin come together and touch. When they're touching, electricity flows from the batteries to the buzzer and the flashlight bulb on the path at the right. This path is called a circuit. As soon as the person stops pressing the doorbell switch, the paper clips move apart. This turns the buzzer and flashlight bulb off by breaking up the path that electricity travels on. Then electricity can no longer flow to the buzzer and flashlight bulb. And that's the shocking truth!

FINISH IT OFF

Make sure nobody will trip over the doorbell wires. Follow the plan you drew to hang the doorbell switch and run its wires along the door frame and baseboards of your room.

1 To hang the doorbell switch, thread the string through the round hinge of the clothespin. Tie a knot in the string to make a loop.

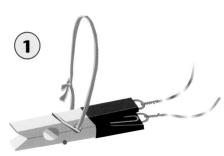

2 Hammer the thumbtack, small nail, or hook into the wall. Hang the loop from it.

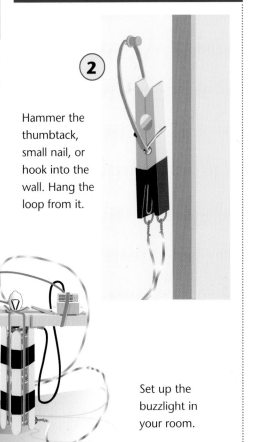

3 Neatly place the long wire along the path you drew. Keep it as close to the door frame and the floor as possible. Hold it in place with clear tape.

4 Set up the buzzlight in your room.

Bouncy Animal

Want to teach an old animal new tricks? Give it a heart, er, "motor transplant" and take it for a walk on a leash. Then you can make it spin like a figure skater or run around in circles all on your command.

Tools & Stuff You Need

- 2 C batteries, 10 Popsicle sticks, 3 elastic bands
- 115 cm (46 in) of speaker wire*
- wire stripper, wire cutters
- X-Acto knife or sharp pointy knife
- small 3-volt DC hobby motor
- mini slide, or toggle, SPST switch*
- small hard rubber or plastic ball
- 2 unpainted metal paper clips
- old hand puppet (you can make one out of a sock) or small stuffed animal
- potato peeler or sharp pointy knife
- 115 cm (46 in) of cord
- electrical tape, 5-minute epoxy glue, scissors, needle, thread, pencil

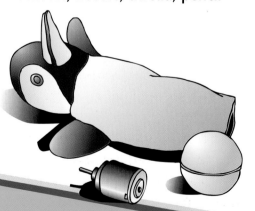

* See page 63 for notes

GEAR UP THE MOTOR

Get the motor ready to put your animal on the move.

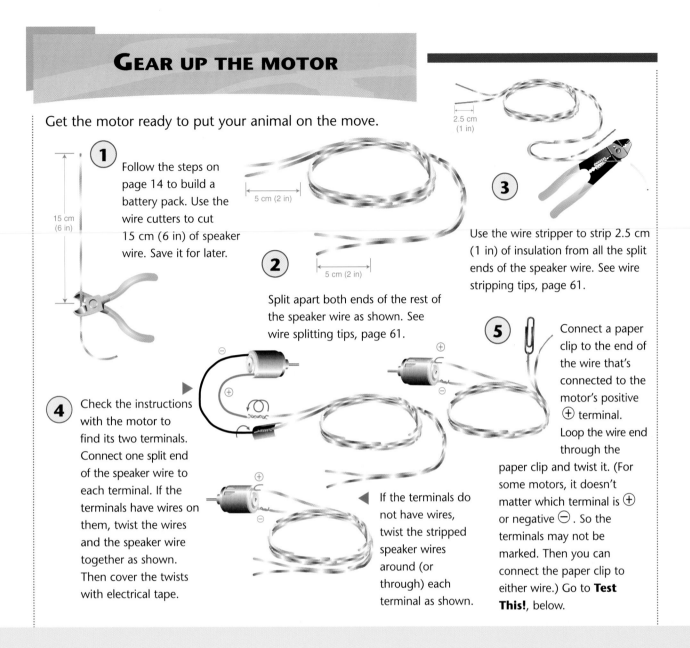

1 Follow the steps on page 14 to build a battery pack. Use the wire cutters to cut 15 cm (6 in) of speaker wire. Save it for later.

15 cm (6 in)

5 cm (2 in)

2 Split apart both ends of the rest of the speaker wire as shown. See wire splitting tips, page 61.

5 cm (2 in)

3 Use the wire stripper to strip 2.5 cm (1 in) of insulation from all the split ends of the speaker wire. See wire stripping tips, page 61.

2.5 cm (1 in)

4 Check the instructions with the motor to find its two terminals. Connect one split end of the speaker wire to each terminal. If the terminals have wires on them, twist the wires and the speaker wire together as shown. Then cover the twists with electrical tape.

If the terminals do not have wires, twist the stripped speaker wires around (or through) each terminal as shown.

5 Connect a paper clip to the end of the wire that's connected to the motor's positive ⊕ terminal. Loop the wire end through the paper clip and twist it. (For some motors, it doesn't matter which terminal is ⊕ or negative ⊖. So the terminals may not be marked. Then you can connect the paper clip to either wire.) Go to **Test This!**, below.

Test This!

- Test your motor and batteries. Take the paper clip, which you just connected to the wire, and slip it under the elastic bands on the ⊕ terminal of the battery pack. Make sure the paper clip makes good contact with the ⊕ terminal.
- Touch the other end of the wire to the ⊖ battery terminal. Does the motor turn? If so, everything is working. Hurray! Skip the next step.
- If not, check that the paper clip is well attached to the wire and that the paper clip is pressing against the metal part of the ⊕ battery terminal. Check that the batteries are pressing against each other. Also, check that the paper clip is metal and not painted. If all the connections look good and the motor still doesn't turn, then the motor or the batteries need to be replaced.
- Disconnect the motor from the battery pack by sliding the paper clip away from the ⊕ terminal.

Get your motor running!

ADD MOTOR POWER

Power up your animal with a "motor transplant."

 Measure the length of a Popsicle stick along your animal to see if the stick will fit inside the animal. If the stick is too long, mark the maximum length that will fit. With the help of an adult, cut 3 Popsicle sticks this long with the X-Acto knife.

 Use the epoxy to glue the Popsicle sticks onto the motor as shown. See epoxy glue tips, page 60.

Secure the wire by taping it to one of the Popsicle sticks.

Use the scissors to cut a hole in the animal as shown. Make the hole big enough for the motor to fit through.

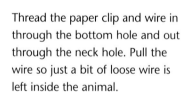

Cut a small hole in the neck of the animal. Make it big enough for a paper clip to fit through.

Thread the paper clip and wire in through the bottom hole and out through the neck hole. Pull the wire so just a bit of loose wire is left inside the animal.

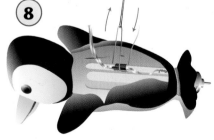

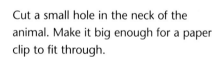 Put the Popsicle sticks and motor into the bottom hole. Push them in so only the end of the motor sticks out. Take some stuffing out of your animal if you need to.

Secure the motor. If possible, put an elastic band around the bottom of the animal as shown. If not, sew loops around the Popsicle sticks through the animal's fur.

GET ON THE BALL

What does it take to get your critter ready to roll? Patience and a steady hand!

1 Have an adult help you use the potato peeler or knife to dig a hole in the ball. Make the hole five times as wide as the motor shaft and a bit deeper than the shaft is long.

2 With an adult, use the potato peeler or knife to make small slits around the hole. The slits will help epoxy glue take grip in the next step.

Put the motor shaft in the hole full of epoxy so a bit of the shaft sticks out. Leave a gap between the bottom of the motor and the ball as shown. Hold the shaft in place for five minutes until the epoxy hardens. Then let it dry for 24 hours before you do the next part.

3 Fill the hole with epoxy glue. Use a Popsicle stick to spread the epoxy around the hole.

4

gap

Start Me Up

Have you ever heard a subway train sing? Believe it or not, subway trains powered by DC motors sing a song every time they start up. The trains need to get going slowly and the voltage, or power, that makes them go has to be stepped up gradually. In order to increase the voltage slowly, parts of a train's circuits switch on and off quickly. As the train speeds up, so does the switching frequency. And this fast switching happens on a frequency you can hear. It's the train's start-up song!

ADD THE CONTROL SWITCH

A simple switch will stop and start your Bouncy Animal.

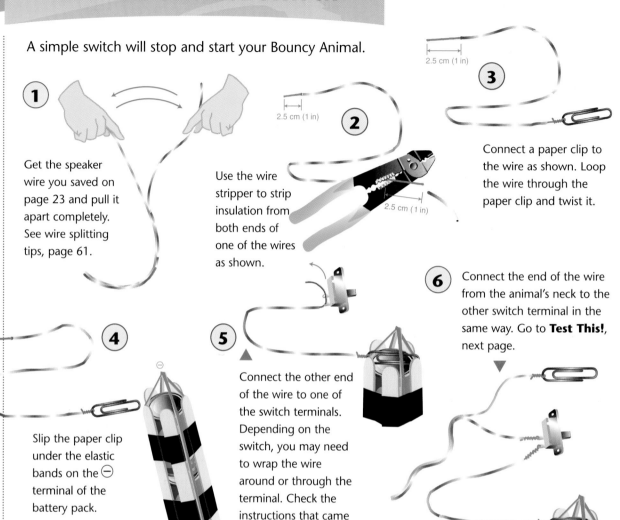

1 Get the speaker wire you saved on page 23 and pull it apart completely. See wire splitting tips, page 61.

2 2.5 cm (1 in) Use the wire stripper to strip insulation from both ends of one of the wires as shown. 2.5 cm (1 in)

3 2.5 cm (1 in) Connect a paper clip to the wire as shown. Loop the wire through the paper clip and twist it.

4 Slip the paper clip under the elastic bands on the ⊖ terminal of the battery pack.

5 Connect the other end of the wire to one of the switch terminals. Depending on the switch, you may need to wrap the wire around or through the terminal. Check the instructions that came with the switch to see what to do.

6 Connect the end of the wire from the animal's neck to the other switch terminal in the same way. Go to **Test This!**, next page.

New Spin on the Taz

Everyone knows that the Tasmanian devil spins like a tornado, right? Wrong! Unlike the whirling cartoon character, the real Taz doesn't spin at all. It jumps quickly from front to back to change directions, but it doesn't spin all the way around. It's called the Tasmanian devil because it lives in Tasmania and is known for having a devilish temper. The Taz has some other "talents," though. It can open its mouth twice as wide as a dog. Its jaws are so strong that the Tasmanian devil can actually eat a whole horse, leaving only the skull and tail!

Time to motor!

Test This!

Test the connections you've just made. Touch the paper clip on the wire from the animal's neck to the ⊕ battery terminal. Does the motor come on? If so, turn the switch to off. If not, check that the switch is turned to on. If the motor comes on now, terrific! Turn it off. If not, check all of the connections. Also, check that the ball and motor shaft spin freely. If they don't, see if they got glued to the motor and scrape away the excess glue with a scissors' blade.

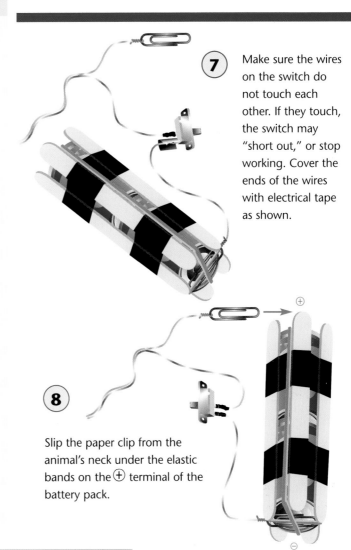

7 Make sure the wires on the switch do not touch each other. If they touch, the switch may "short out," or stop working. Cover the ends of the wires with electrical tape as shown.

8 Slip the paper clip from the animal's neck under the elastic bands on the ⊕ terminal of the battery pack.

FINISHING TOUCHES

Put a leash on your animal and take it for a spin.

1

Use the epoxy to glue the switch on the battery pack.

2

Don't use the wires as a leash or you could pull apart the connections. Instead, tie a cord around the animal's neck. Twist the wires around the cord, leaving the wires a bit loose inside the animal. Then tie the cord around the battery pack. (See p. 22 top.)

How to
Go for a Spin

Whee!

(1) Place your critter on the floor. Hold the leash so the critter stands tall and the ball touches the floor (it won't work well on carpet).

(2) If part of the leash is left over, wrap it around the battery pack.

(3) Turn the switch on. If the motor doesn't spin, hold your critter in the air and spin the ball lightly with your hand to start the motor as shown below. DC motors start slowly and, at times, they need something to give them a spin to get up to speed. Keep spinning the ball until the motor is turning fast.

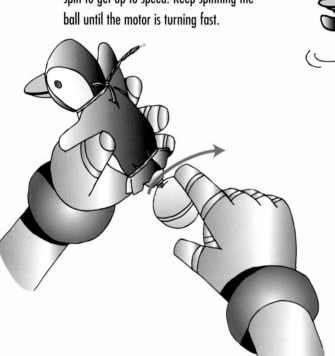

(5) Let your critter unwind every now and then. Turn it off, hold it in the air by the leash, and let it spin to unwind the leash.

(4) Play around. Hold the leash so your critter stands up at different angles. Have your critter stand up straight and watch it spin on the spot like a figure skater. Tilt it and watch it run circles around you like a puppy.

Zoom In
on the Mechanics

Different motors need different amounts of electricity to run. The DC motor that spins your animal around runs on 3 volts of electricity. This electricity comes from the 3-volt battery pack that you connected to the motor. (The battery pack is made out of two 1.5-volt C batteries. Since the batteries are connected, their power gets added together to make 3 volts of electricity.) The switch you connected to the motor allows you to turn the motor on and off easily. When you turn it on, electricity flows from the battery to the motor, along a path called a circuit (see right). Then the motor turns the ball and your critter goes for a spin!

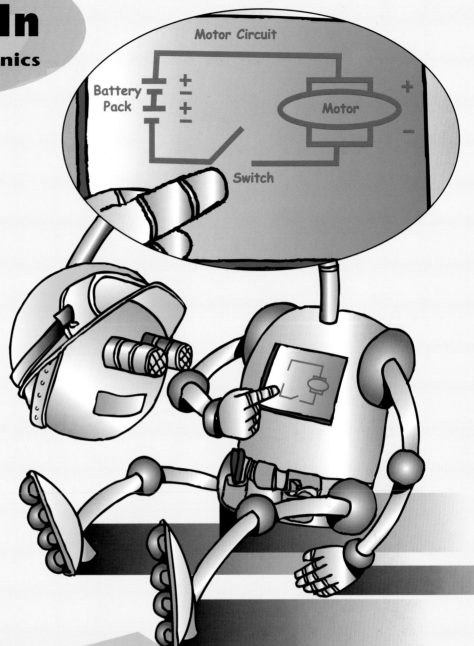

Motor Circuit

Battery Pack

Motor

Switch

Surf the Web

The motor in your Bouncy Animal is small compared to a car motor. But compared to a micromotor, it's a giant. Micromotors are so tiny they can fit on the head of a pin! Experts think doctors will use micromotors for things like driving mirrors through the human body to get the inside scoop on their patients. Then there are the nanomotors, which are even 100 times tinier than micromotors. They may be used to replace cells, or tiny building blocks, of the human body. To find out more about small motors, do a keyword search for "micromotor" and "nanomotor" in a search engine on the Internet.

Secret Code Machine

Want to send a message to your friends that no one else can read? Build the Secret Code Machine. Not only can it encode and decode messages, it can also become a quiz game (see page 43). Here's what you need for one machine. But you and your friends may want to make one each to read each other's messages!

Tools & Stuff You Need

- safety goggles
- pencil, 21.5 x 28 cm ($8\frac{1}{2}$ x 11 in) graph paper, 60 paper clips, 108 blank labels or sticker dots, 4 old marker caps the same size, 27 rubber hair elastics, Scotch tape, electrical tape
- 2 C batteries, 10 Popsicle sticks, 2 large elastic bands, aluminum pie plate, scissors, 5-minute epoxy glue
- wood blocks or work bench, saw, hammer, screwdriver, wire cutters

- wire stripper, drill with 2.7- or 3-mm ($\frac{7}{64}$ or $\frac{1}{8}$ in) bit, clamp, sandpaper, paint, paintbrush
- 27 LEDs 2 to 3 volts with long leads
- carbon film resistor about 22 ohms
- 54 machine screws 2 cm ($\frac{3}{4}$ in) long size 4*, 54 nuts size 4*, 4 wood screws 1.3 cm ($\frac{1}{2}$ in) long size 4*, 108 washers size 4 or 6*
- 29 common nails 2 cm ($\frac{3}{4}$ in) long*, small nail 2.5 cm (1 in) long*
- plywood 20 x 44 cm (8 x $17\frac{1}{4}$ in), 9 mm ($\frac{3}{8}$ in) thick
- 4 m (13 ft) of speaker wire*

* See page 63 for notes

BUILD THE CODE BOARD

Roll up your sleeves and get to work on your Secret Code Machine. Ask an adult to help you with steps 2 to 4.

Building la secret coda!

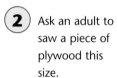

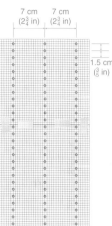

1 Plan the board. On graph paper, draw 3 columns of 27 dots each as you see here.

2 Ask an adult to saw a piece of plywood this size.

20 cm (8 in)

44 cm (17¼ in)

height/depth of board: 9 mm (⅜ in)

3 **Wear safety goggles for steps 3 and 4.**

Center the plan on top of the board and tape it in place. Ask the adult to drill a hole in the board at each dot.

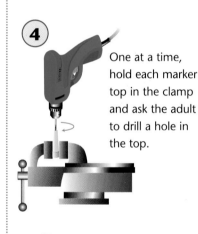

4 One at a time, hold each marker top in the clamp and ask the adult to drill a hole in the top.

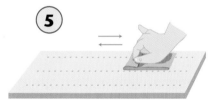

5 Sand the holes and edges of the board with sandpaper to remove all the loose wood bits from both sides of the board.

6 Paint both sides of the board and let it dry.

007 Goes to School

In England in 1939, a special school was set up for math and language experts, spy novel writers, chess masters, and professors to learn about breaking codes. Ian Fleming, the author of the James Bond novels, went there. The school was called the Government Code and Cypher School. But it was nicknamed the Golf, Cheese, and Chess Society!

THE NAME IS BOND JAMES BOND

BOARD THE POWER BUS

Go electric: put your wooden board on a power bus.

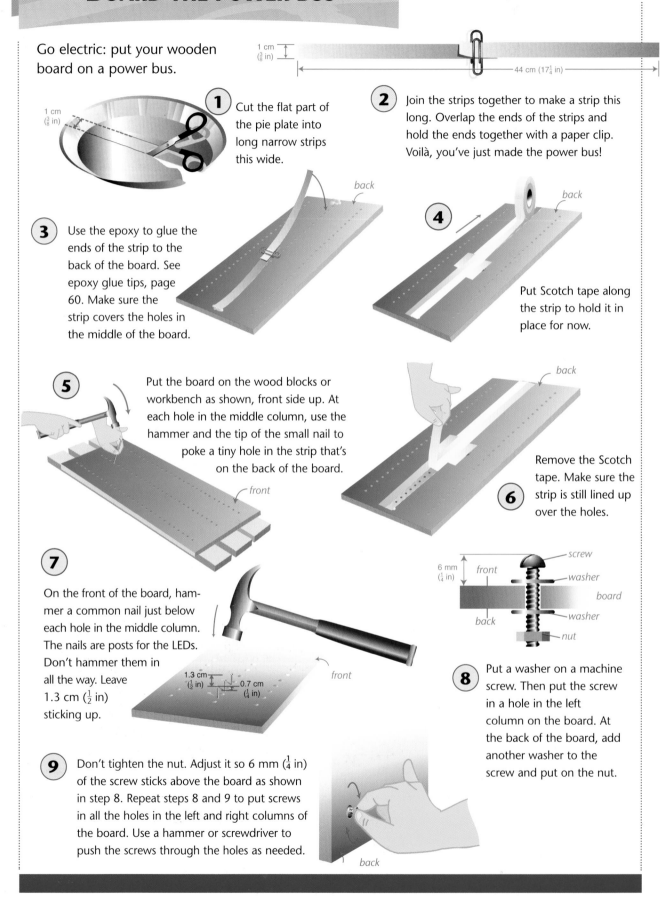

1 Cut the flat part of the pie plate into long narrow strips this wide.

1 cm (3/8 in)

2 Join the strips together to make a strip this long. Overlap the ends of the strips and hold the ends together with a paper clip. Voilà, you've just made the power bus!

1 cm (3/8 in)   44 cm (17¼ in)

3 Use the epoxy to glue the ends of the strip to the back of the board. See epoxy glue tips, page 60. Make sure the strip covers the holes in the middle of the board.

back

4 Put Scotch tape along the strip to hold it in place for now.

back

5 Put the board on the wood blocks or workbench as shown, front side up. At each hole in the middle column, use the hammer and the tip of the small nail to poke a tiny hole in the strip that's on the back of the board.

front

6 Remove the Scotch tape. Make sure the strip is still lined up over the holes.

back

7 On the front of the board, hammer a common nail just below each hole in the middle column. The nails are posts for the LEDs. Don't hammer them in all the way. Leave 1.3 cm (½ in) sticking up.

1.3 cm (½ in)   0.7 cm (¼ in)   front

8 Put a washer on a machine screw. Then put the screw in a hole in the left column on the board. At the back of the board, add another washer to the screw and put on the nut.

6 mm (¼ in)   front   screw   washer   board   back   washer   nut

9 Don't tighten the nut. Adjust it so 6 mm (¼ in) of the screw sticks above the board as shown in step 8. Repeat steps 8 and 9 to put screws in all the holes in the left and right columns of the board. Use a hammer or screwdriver to push the screws through the holes as needed.

back

Gear up the board with a power pack and a "magic" wand.

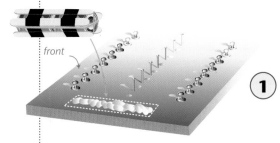

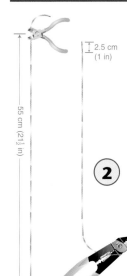

2.5 cm
(1 in)

55 cm (21½ in)

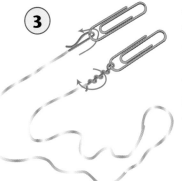

front

1 Turn to page 14 to build a battery pack out of Popsicle sticks. Spread epoxy glue on the board as shown to glue the battery pack on the board.

2 Split the speaker wire into two wires by pulling it apart completely. See wire splitting tips, page 61. Then use the wire cutters to cut a piece of wire 55 cm (21½ in) long. Use the wire strippers to strip 2.5 cm (1 in) of insulation from both ends.

3 Connect each wire end to a paper clip. Loop the end through the paper clip and twist it.

4 Slip one paper clip under the elastic bands on the negative ⊖ battery terminal. The other paper clip is the secret code wand.

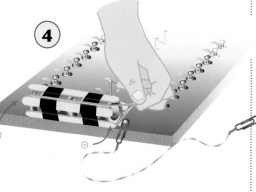

Cracking the Enigma Code

In World War II, the German army encoded and decoded secret messages with a special machine that looked like an old-fashioned typewriter. It was called the "Enigma Machine." As the letters of a message were typed in, they came out in code. Each message included an encryption key like the key, or order of the letters on the right side of your Secret Code Machine. The key told the receiver how to set his or her Enigma Machine to decode the message. The Germans said the Enigma coding system was so complicated that it would take 1000 people working on Enigma Machines 900 million years to crack it. But maybe they were bluffing. With help from spies, Polish math experts soon cracked the code, and the Allies began decoding German messages to find out the Germans' plans. Then the fact that the experts had cracked the code became one of the most important and well-kept secrets of the war.

$\sqrt{x+y} = 2x$

E_c

$M \times x \, 2 = ??$

TURN DOWN THE POWER

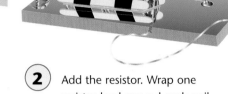

The battery pack pumps out too much power for some LEDs to handle. Add a resistor to cut down the power.

① 1 *front* Hammer two common nails into the board beside the positive ⊕ terminal of the battery pack as shown.

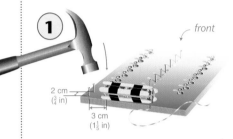

2 cm (¾ in)
3 cm (1⅕ in)

② 2 Add the resistor. Wrap one resistor lead around each nail.

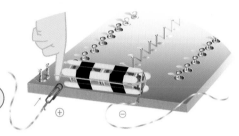

③ 3 Use the wire cutters to cut a piece of wire 8 cm (3⅛ in). Use the wire stripper to strip 2.5 cm (1 in) of insulation from both ends.

8 cm (3⅛ in)

2.5 cm (1 in)

④ 4 Loop one end through a paper clip and twist it. Slip the paper clip under the elastic bands on the ⊕ battery terminal.

⊕   ⊖

back

⑤ 5 Wrap the other end around the nail shown.

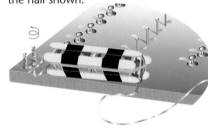

⑥ 6 Cut and strip the ends of a wire 8 cm (3⅛ in) long as in step 3 above. Wrap one end around the other nail as shown.

⑦ 7 Loop the other end of the wire through a paper clip and twist it. Attach the paper clip to the aluminum strip on the back of the board.

Seen Any Scrambled TV Lately?

Chances are some of your favorite TV shows are broadcast in scrambled codes. In fact, you may have a decoding machine hooked up to your TV that unscrambles these TV signals before they hit the tube. Several channels and networks scramble, or encode, their broadcast signals, so you can't see their shows unless you have paid to watch them and have their decoding machine. Sneaky stuff!

Test This!

- Test all the LEDs to see if they're working. Check the LED package to figure out which lead is ⊖. (Often, it's the shorter of the two leads.) Use the pliers to bend the ⊖ lead, so it makes a right angle with the ⊕ lead as shown in step 1 below.
- Touch the ⊕ lead to the resistor nail that is connected to the power bus, and touch the ⊖ lead to the wand from the ⊖ battery terminal. Does the LED light up? If so, everything's cool. Skip the next two steps and test the rest of the LEDs the same way.
- If not, make sure all the connections on the paper clips, resistor, and battery pack are secure and the ⊖ LED lead is touching the paper clip of the wand. Also, make sure the batteries are touching each other.
- If the LED still doesn't light up, the LED or the batteries aren't working. Test another LED to figure out which.
- Got all the LEDs working? Test the power bus. Touch the ⊕ lead of one LED to the power bus, and touch the ⊖ lead to the wand from the ⊖ battery terminal. Does the LED light up? If so, repeat this test at several spots along the power bus to make sure power flows throughout the whole bus.
- If not, check the connections on the power bus, resistor, and battery pack. Make sure the metal of the paper clip and aluminum strip are touching. Also, make sure the strips of the power bus are touching.

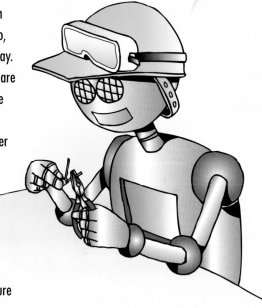

Hey, Mechano Kid! Test the lights before you wire 'em up below.

LIGHT IT UP!

Do the **Test This!** above and then add the LEDs to the board.

1 Bend the ⊖ LED lead as shown. Put the ⊕ lead through a hole in the board and the corresponding hole in the power bus. Push the LED down so it sits on top of the hole.

⊖   ⊕

front

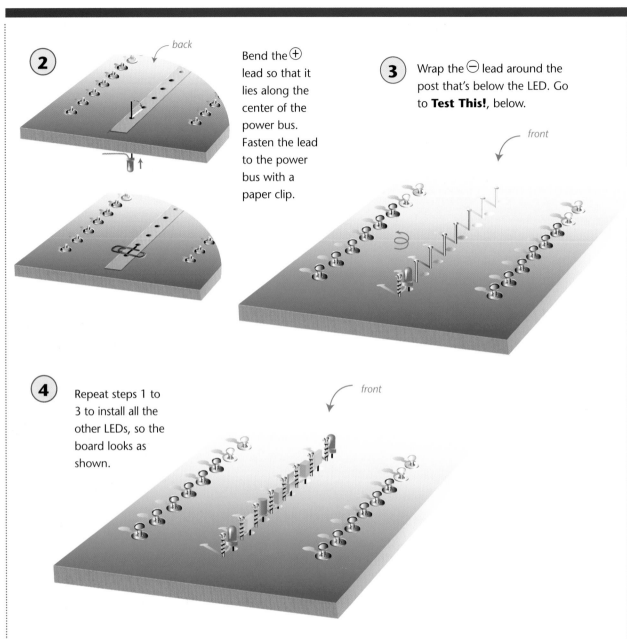

2 Bend the ⊕ lead so that it lies along the center of the power bus. Fasten the lead to the power bus with a paper clip.

3 Wrap the ⊖ lead around the post that's below the LED. Go to **Test This!**, below.

4 Repeat steps 1 to 3 to install all the other LEDs, so the board looks as shown.

Test This!

Test the LED you've just hooked up. Touch the post with the wand. Does the LED light up? If so, way to go! If not, check the connections and make sure the LED lead didn't break. Test each LED like this once you've added it to the board.

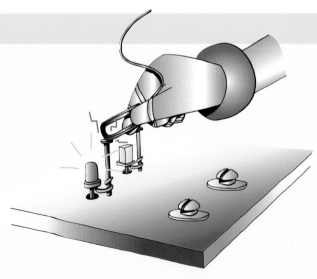

MAKE THE CODING SWITCHES

Switch things up so you can encode and decode messages.

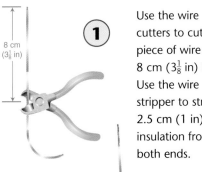

8 cm (3⅛ in)

1 Use the wire cutters to cut a piece of wire 8 cm (3⅛ in) long. Use the wire stripper to strip 2.5 cm (1 in) of insulation from both ends.

2.5 cm (1 in)

2 Connect one end to the small end of a paper clip. Loop and twist it around the paper clip.

3 Slip a hair elastic onto the small end of the paper clip, so it hangs as shown.

Wrap the free end of the wire around the last LED post on the board.

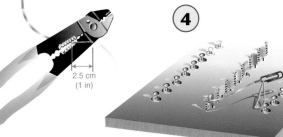

4

5 Slip the hair elastic over the post. Loop the big end of the paper clip around the screw on the right side of the board. Go to **Test This!**, below.

6 Repeat these steps to make 26 more coding switches. Test each one as you go. (When the coding switches are on the right side of the board as shown, you can ENCODE messages. When they are on the left side, you can DECODE messages.)

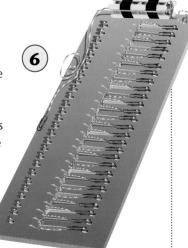

Test This!

Test the coding switch you've just made. Touch the screw with the wand. If the LED lights up, kudos — it's working perfectly! If not, check that all of the connections are made well and that the stripped wire is wrapped around the post and the paper clip. Remember, this will work only with metal paper clips. Plastic and painted paper clips do not conduct electricity.

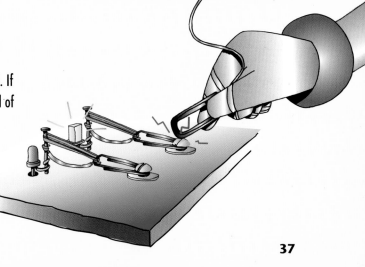

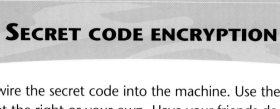

Hard-wire the secret code into the machine. Use the robot's code at the right or your own. Have your friends do exactly the same wiring, so you can read each other's messages.

1 Write the alphabet on the sticker dots or labels. Use them to label each of the screws on the left side of the board. Add a period for the last screw. Label each of the screws on the right side in the same way, but in the reverse order. Put an "ENCODE" label on the left and a "DECODE" label on the right.

front

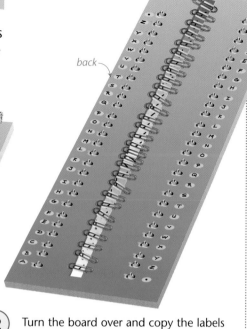

back

2 Turn the board over and copy the labels onto the back of the board. Make sure each screw on the back is labeled the same way as it is on the front.

3 Stretch some wire between A and F exactly as shown. Use the wire cutters to cut the wire so it is 3 cm ($1\frac{1}{5}$ in) longer than the distance between the letters.

3 cm
($1\frac{1}{5}$ in)

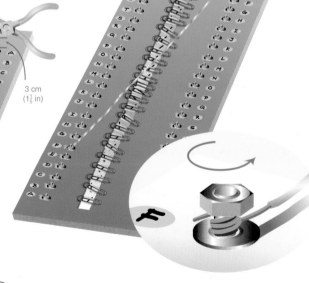

4 Use the wire stripper to strip 2.5 cm (1 in) from each end. On the back of the board, connect A to F by wrapping the stripped ends of the wire around the screws between the nuts and the washers. Go to **Test This!**, right.

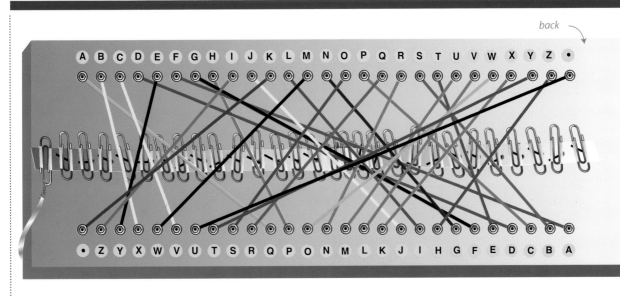

5 Repeat steps 3 and 4 to encrypt, or code, the rest of the letters as in the robot's list. Go to **Test This!**, below, to test each one as you go.

Test This!

Test the encryption wiring you've just hooked up. On the front of the board, touch the A on the ENCODE side with the secret code wand. Does the F light on the DECODE side light up? If so, code away! If not, check the connections. Make sure that the wire on the back of the board connects the letter A on the ENCODE side to F on the DECODE side. Also, make sure all the coding switches are hooked on the right side of the board. If it still doesn't light up, check if the F light is working by touching the post at F with the wand. If it doesn't light up now, check the LED and power bus connections. But if it does light up, touch the F screw with the wand. If it doesn't light up this time, the F coding switch has fallen apart and needs to be reconnected.

Secret Code Connect:	G to N	N to R	U to .
A to F	H to Z	O to W	V to C
B to S	I to L	P to H	W to M
C to P	J to J	Q to A	X to B
D to D	K to X	R to Q	Y to E
E to T	L to V	S to O	Z to I
F to G	M to U	T to Y	. to K

Your board is almost ready for action. Just do these steps to keep your connections in good working order.

front

1 Add legs to the board. Put a wood screw in the hole in each of the four marker tops. On the back of the board, use the screwdriver to attach one marker top to each corner.

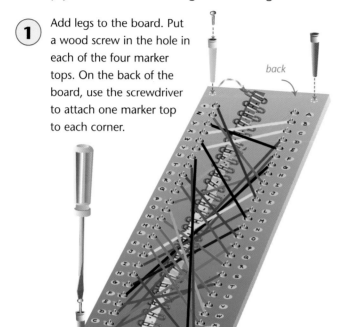

back

2 When you're not using the Secret Code Machine, wrap the wand wire around the battery pack. Fasten the paper clip on the wand to an elastic band on the battery pack. This will stop the wand from accidentally hooking onto a screw, or connection post, and burning out the batteries or LEDs.

Change the Code

Think someone's onto your code? Don't panic. Change it!

Quick 'n' Easy Method

Once the board is hard-wired, the letters on the right side of the board are a key for the code. They light up to show what each letter of the alphabet is coded as. So you can change this code by changing the key, or the order of these letters. Just peel off the letter labels or stickers and stick them back in a different order. Don't forget to tell your friends the new order, so they can label their boards exactly the same way. Otherwise, they won't be able to read your messages. Send the new key (order of the letters) as a separate message or as the beginning of a new message.

Tough to Crack Method

Hard-wiring a new code into your machine will make your code tougher for hackers to crack. (If you don't change the wiring, a good hacker will eventually figure it out. Then he or she will be able to read any message you send that includes a key!) Get together with your friends and decide on a new encryption plan. Remove all the wires from the back of the boards and follow the instructions in the Secret Code Encryption section to hard-wire the boards according to your new plan. Rewire all of your boards exactly the same way, or else you won't be able to decode each other's messages.

How to
Encode and Decode Secret Messages

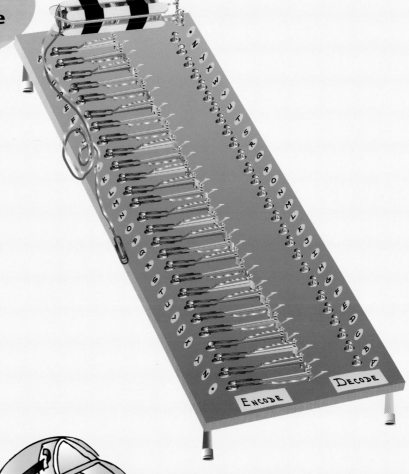

1 To encode a secret message, write it out on a piece of paper first.

2 Set the Secret Code Machine to ENCODE mode. Loop all the paper clips of the coding switches onto the screws on the right side of the board as shown in step 1 on p. 38.

3 For each letter in the message, touch the secret code wand to the screw beside the letter on the ENCODE side of the board. Then the LED next to the coded letter on the other side of the board should light up. Say you were encoding the name Rachel, for example. If you followed the robot's code to hard-wire the board, you would touch:
R and Q would light up
A and F would light up
C and P would light up
H and Z would light up
E and T would light up
L and V would light up
That means that RACHEL would be encoded as QFPZTV.

4 On another piece of paper, write down the encoded letters and send this message to your friends. (The period will come in handy if your message has a few sentences.)

5 To decode a secret message, set the Secret Code Machine to DECODE mode. Loop all the paper clips of the coding switches onto the screws on the left side of the board as shown above.

6 For each letter in the secret message, touch the secret code wand to the screw beside the letter on the DECODE side of the board. Then the LED next to the coded letter on the other side of the board should light up. Write down these letters to decode the message.

7 Do steps 5 and 6 to decode the message on the robot's chest. Check your answer on page 64.

Zoom In
on the Mechanics

Connection Post

A

Back of board encryption

Secret Code Wand

3v Battery Pack

22Ω Resistor

LED

Power Bus

Decode Encode Switch

F

You are writing a secret message for your best friend's eyes only. You touch the secret code wand to the letter A in the message and the coded letter F lights up instantly. How does the Secret Code Machine do it? When you hard-wired the board, you built in the code by connecting A to F at the back of the board. This allows power, or electricity, to flow from A to F to light F up.

In order to flow, electricity must travel in a loop or circuit. Here's how it flows in the circuit between A and F (see above). When the board is in ENCODE mode, all the coding switches are hooked up to the coding key on the right side of the board.

So F is connected to the ⊖ LED lead of the light next to it. The ⊕ lead of this LED is connected to the aluminum strip, or "power bus," at the back of the board. And the power bus is connected, through the resistor, to the ⊕ battery terminal.

Now all that is needed to complete the circuit between A and F is to connect the ⊖ battery terminal to A. And that's exactly what happens when you encode A by touching the secret code wand to A.

Presto! The circuit is complete, electricity flows through it, and the LED beside F lights up!

Surf the Web

Want to find more information about making and breaking codes and the Enigma Machine? Do a keyword search for "secret code" and "enigma machine" in some search engines on the Net.

42

Quiz Game

Hey, quizmaster! Want to host your own game show? Here's your chance. Think up some great questions and answers. Make the Quiz Game, gather your friends, and let the show begin!

It's two gadgets in one! Quiz Game turns into Secret Code Machine and vice versa because they use the same mechanics.

Tools & Stuff **You Need**

- paper hole punch, scissors, 6 paper clips, marker, large index cards or Bristol™ board
- Secret Code Machine or the tools and stuff on page 30

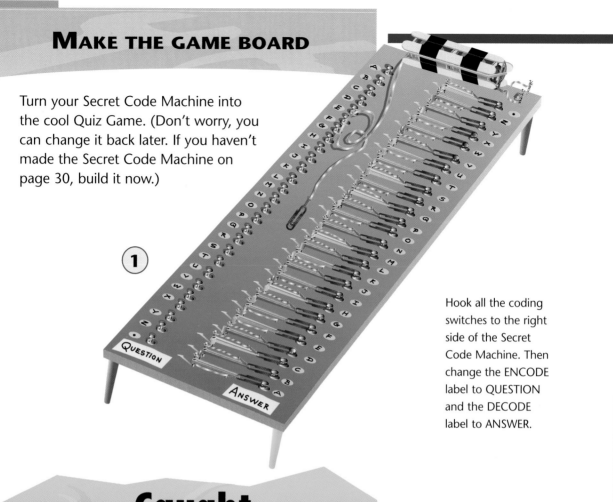

Turn your Secret Code Machine into the cool Quiz Game. (Don't worry, you can change it back later. If you haven't made the Secret Code Machine on page 30, build it now.)

(1)

Hook all the coding switches to the right side of the Secret Code Machine. Then change the ENCODE label to QUESTION and the DECODE label to ANSWER.

Cheaters **Caught** in the **Act**

Quiz shows became all the rage on TV in the late 1950s. That's when quiz shows began to give away big bucks as prizes. Some of them like "The $64,000 Question" were so popular that families planned their schedules around watching them. Unfortunately, some TV producers figured even more people would watch the shows if the winners were people with good TV personalities — not people who could answer the questions correctly.
So the producers "fixed" the winners by secretly telling them the answers to the questions. In 1958, a losing player realized this and the producers were charged with cheating. People stopped watching quiz shows in disgust. In fact, it took about 10 years for the shows to become popular again!

BRAINSTORM QUESTIONS AND ANSWERS

The game board handles six questions at a time. But you'll want more than that to keep the game going.

1

Use the scissors to cut six strips as above from the index cards or Bristol™ board. Punch a hole in each strip as you see here.

2 cm ($\frac{3}{4}$ in)

1 cm ($\frac{3}{8}$ in)

15 cm (6 in)

2 Think of six tough questions. Write one on each strip. Or input them on a computer, print them, cut them out, and glue them on the strips. But don't cover the holes.

3 Cut 24 strips this size from the index cards or Bristol™ board. Punch a hole in each strip as shown.

2 cm ($\frac{3}{4}$ in)

1 cm ($\frac{3}{8}$ in)

10 cm (4 in)

4

What city does Batman live in?
What's the capital of Canada?
Who's the author of the U.P...
How many volts are in a C battery?
"Stop Right Now"?

Write the answers to the questions on these strips. For each question, also think of three "close but wrong" answers. Write all the wrong answers on the 18 remaining strips.

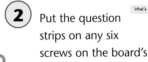

Vancouver

SET UP THE BOARD

What's the capital of Can...

Fasten your seatbelts, er, questions and fire up the game board.

What's the name of Mickey Mouse's dog?

1 Put a paper clip on the end of each question strip. Make sure the big end of it overlaps the hole on the strip as shown.

2 Put the question strips on any six screws on the board's left side. Slip the holes over the screws. Then secure the strips by lightly pulling them, so the paper clips hook onto the screws.

3 Touch the wand to each screw that holds a question. Check which letter on the right side of the board lights up. Slip the correct answer strip on the screw at this letter. Clip the end of the strip to the paper clip there.

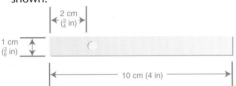

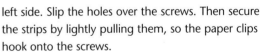

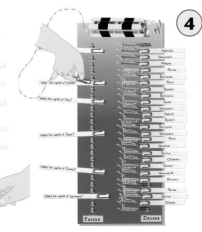

4 Put the 18 "close but wrong" answers on the other screws on the right side of the board in any order. A few screws will be left empty. Leave them blank or make silly answers to put on them.

How to Play
the Quiz Game

1 The person who made up the questions plays the quizmaster who asks the questions. (After all, he or she knows all the answers!) The other players play game show contestants.

2 The quizmaster asks a question and the contestants call out the answer as fast as they can.

3 After all the contestants have given an answer, the quizmaster touches the wand to the question to make the right answer light up. The contestant who said the right answer first wins a point.

4 Play through the rest of the questions the same way. The contestant with the most points wins.

5 Make the game your own. Change the rules, write new questions, or set up the board with 27 questions and 27 answers. The only rule is to have fun!

Idea that Switched
the World

In 1936, math expert Alan Turing had a strange idea that changed the world. The idea was that most difficult problems could be solved by following simple instructions. To prove his idea, he wanted to build intelligent machines that could understand simple instructions and be programmed to do different things rather than big, complicated machines that could do only one thing. The simple instructions would be carried out by on and off switches. Turing's idea became known as the "Turing Machine," and it led to the first programmable computer. Today, most computers are made of millions of switches. The Quiz Game and the Secret Code Machine work with lots of switches, too. In fact, turning the Secret Code Machine into the Quiz Game is like changing the machine's program!

Alarm in a Box

Is your little brother driving you crazy by always getting into your stuff? Want to stash some things in a safe place? Make this Alarm in a Box. Unless you disarm it with a secret code that only you know, it'll go off whenever anyone opens it — bzzzzt!

Tools & Stuff You Need

- safety goggles, scissors, needle-nose pliers, wire cutters, wire stripper, tape measure, screwdriver, X-Acto or sharp knife, drill with a 3-mm ($\frac{1}{8}$ in) bit
- a baby wipes box or similar container with a hinged top (see approximate size below)
- 2 C batteries, white film container with a top that turns easily
- 10 Popsicle sticks, 2 large elastic bands, 2 paper clips, 2 thumbtacks, aluminum pie plate, bottle cork
- thin cardboard 21.5 x 28 cm ($8\frac{1}{2}$ x 11 in), pencil, marker

- 1.5 m (5 ft) of thin solid-core hobby wire or 22 to 24 gauge wire
- 3-volt DC buzzer "normally off"
- bobby pin ("professional" quality), electrical tape, contact cement
- metal spring 2.5 cm (1 in) long (like those in pens)
- 2 machine screws 1.3 cm ($\frac{1}{2}$ in) long size 5*, 2 nuts size 5*, flat-head wood screw 3.8 cm ($1\frac{1}{2}$ in) long size 5*

12 cm (5 in)

20 cm (8 in)

14 cm ($5\frac{1}{2}$ in)

* See page 63 for size notes

Electricity makes the alarm buzz. It flows from the battery to the buzzer on a path called a circuit. So get building!

Power your box with a battery pack.

1

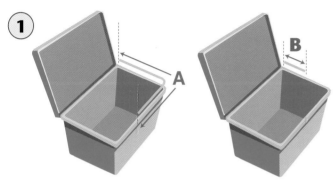

Follow the steps on page 14 to build a battery pack with Popsicle sticks. Measure the parts of the box marked A and B. Use the wire cutters to cut one piece of wire 8 cm ($3\frac{1}{8}$ in) longer than A and another piece 8 cm ($3\frac{1}{8}$ in) longer than B.

2

2.5 cm (1 in)

Use the wire stripper to strip 2.5 cm (1 in) of insulation from the ends of the wires and the buzzer wires. See wire stripping tips, page 61.

2.5 cm (1 in)

3

Connect one end of the short wire to a paper clip. Loop the wire through the paper clip and then twist it.

4

Slip the paper clip under the elastic bands on the negative ⊖ terminal of the battery pack as you see here.

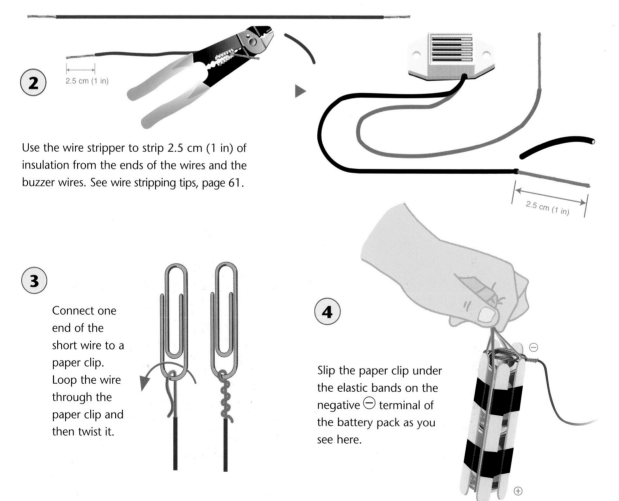

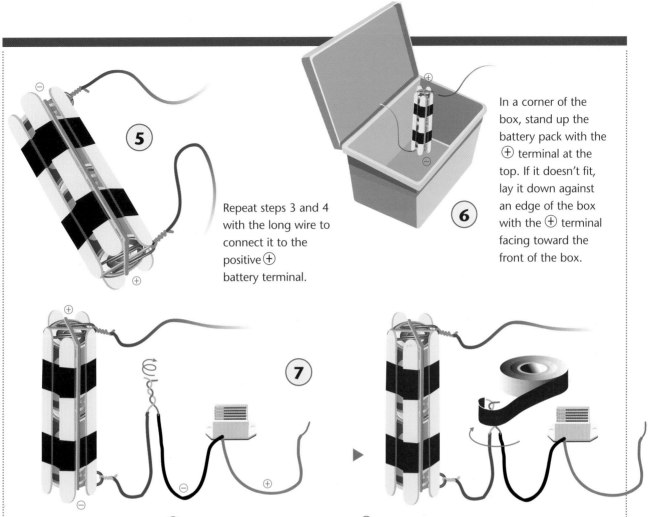

5

Repeat steps 3 and 4 with the long wire to connect it to the positive ⊕ battery terminal.

6

In a corner of the box, stand up the battery pack with the ⊕ terminal at the top. If it doesn't fit, lay it down against an edge of the box with the ⊕ terminal facing toward the front of the box.

7

Connect the wire from the ⊖ terminal of the battery pack to the ⊖ terminal of the buzzer, which is usually black. See connecting wires tips, page 60, and check out any instructions that came with the buzzer. Cover the twist with electrical tape. Go to **Test This!**, below.

Test This!

Stop! Before you go any further, test the buzzer. Take the end of the wire from the ⊕ terminal of the battery pack and touch it to the ⊕ terminal of the buzzer, which is usually red. If it buzzes, hooray — you've got the buzzer working! If it doesn't, check that all the wires are well connected. If it still doesn't work, test the batteries by using them to do something else. If there's still no buzzing, you may have a broken buzzer on your hands that needs to be replaced.

If you hear a buzz, your connections are A-OK!

BUZZZZ!!

ADD THE SECRET CODE SWITCH

Make a film container lid into a secret code switch — a dial with a secret number that turns the alarm on and off.

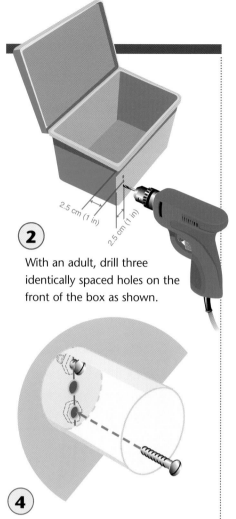

1 On the bottom of the film container, draw a line through the center. With an adult to help, drill three holes on the line as shown.

3 mm (⅛ in) 3 mm (⅛ in)

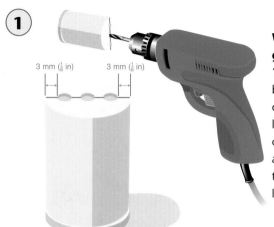

Wear safety goggles for steps 1 and 2.

2 With an adult, drill three identically spaced holes on the front of the box as shown.

2.5 cm (1 in) 2.5 cm (1 in)

3 Glue the container bottom to the front of the box with contact cement. See contact cement tips, page 59. Before you stick it on, line up the holes in the container with those on the box.

4 Secure the film container. Put the two machine screws in the holes as shown. Put the nuts on the screws inside the box and tighten them with your fingers.

Switches Are Everywhere

What makes your Alarm in a Box buzz on and off? Two electric switches — a box top switch and a secret code switch. When the box is opened, the box top switch turns the buzzer on. The secret code switch turns the buzzer off. Electric switches are everywhere — on lights, radios, CD players, toys, and burglar alarms. There are lots of hidden ones, too, like the switches that are major building blocks of computers. But no matter what a switch looks like, its job is to turn something on or off. When an electric switch is on, it allows electricity to flow. When it is off, it stops electricity from flowing. Flip a switch and go with the flow!

RIG UP THE SECRET CODE SWITCH

Get into the nitty-gritty of secret code mechanics.

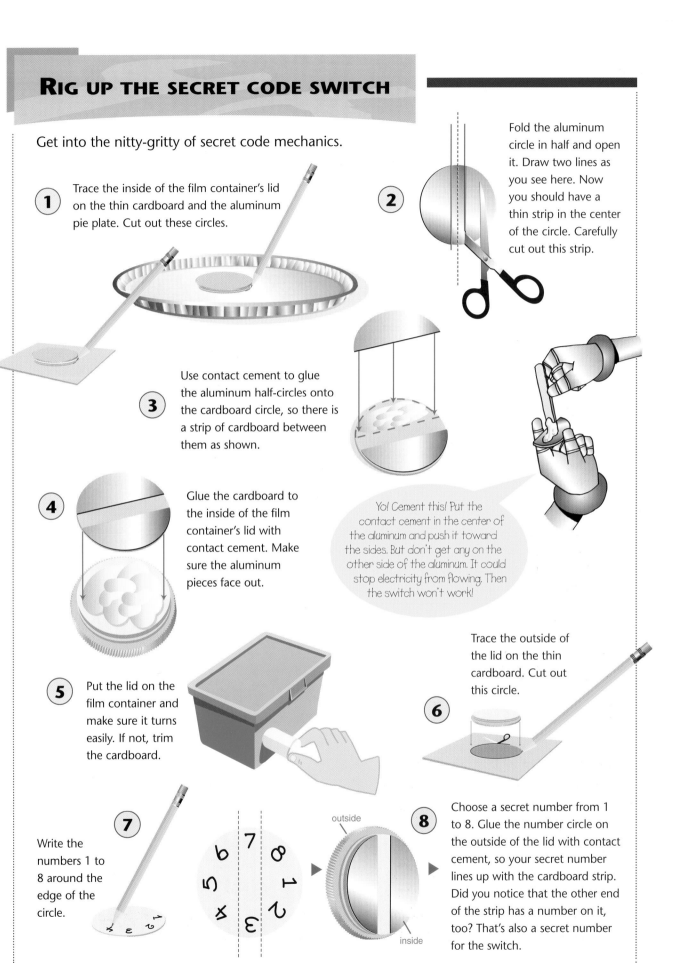

1 Trace the inside of the film container's lid on the thin cardboard and the aluminum pie plate. Cut out these circles.

2 Fold the aluminum circle in half and open it. Draw two lines as you see here. Now you should have a thin strip in the center of the circle. Carefully cut out this strip.

3 Use contact cement to glue the aluminum half-circles onto the cardboard circle, so there is a strip of cardboard between them as shown.

Yo! Cement this! Put the contact cement in the center of the aluminum and push it toward the sides. But don't get any on the other side of the aluminum. It could stop electricity from flowing. Then the switch won't work!

4 Glue the cardboard to the inside of the film container's lid with contact cement. Make sure the aluminum pieces face out.

5 Put the lid on the film container and make sure it turns easily. If not, trim the cardboard.

6 Trace the outside of the lid on the thin cardboard. Cut out this circle.

7 Write the numbers 1 to 8 around the edge of the circle.

outside

inside

8 Choose a secret number from 1 to 8. Glue the number circle on the outside of the lid with contact cement, so your secret number lines up with the cardboard strip. Did you notice that the other end of the strip has a number on it, too? That's also a secret number for the switch.

WIRE UP THE SECRET CODE SWITCH

You are about to connect the switch to the buzzer.

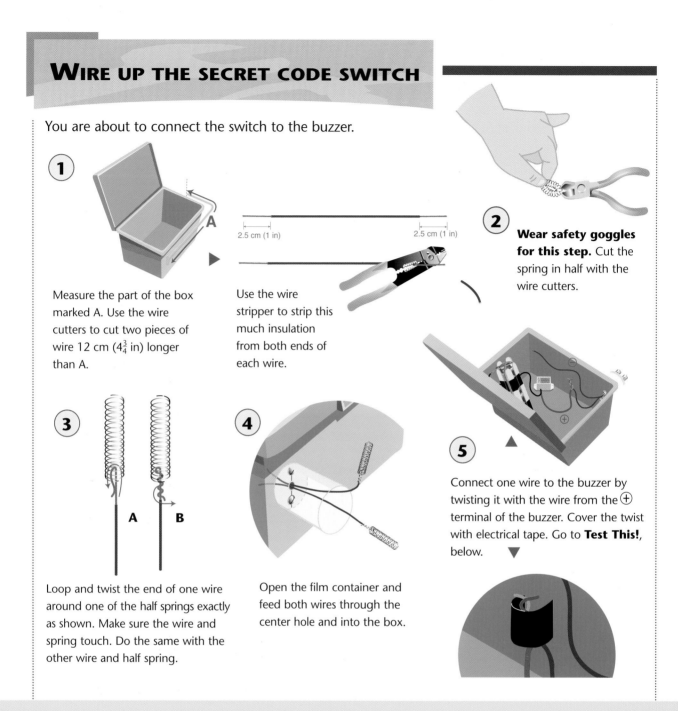

1 Measure the part of the box marked A. Use the wire cutters to cut two pieces of wire 12 cm ($4\frac{3}{4}$ in) longer than A.

2.5 cm (1 in)   2.5 cm (1 in)

Use the wire stripper to strip this much insulation from both ends of each wire.

2 **Wear safety goggles for this step.** Cut the spring in half with the wire cutters.

3 Loop and twist the end of one wire around one of the half springs exactly as shown. Make sure the wire and spring touch. Do the same with the other wire and half spring.

A   B

4 Open the film container and feed both wires through the center hole and into the box.

5 Connect one wire to the buzzer by twisting it with the wire from the ⊕ terminal of the buzzer. Cover the twist with electrical tape. Go to **Test This!**, below.

Test This!

You've just made several electrical connections. Are they working? Test 'em out. Lightly pinch the springs together, between your thumb and index finger, so they're touching. With your other hand, take the wire that's not connected to the buzzer and touch it to the ⊕ terminal wire of the battery pack. Do you hear a buzz? If not, check that all the wires are well connected and try this test again.

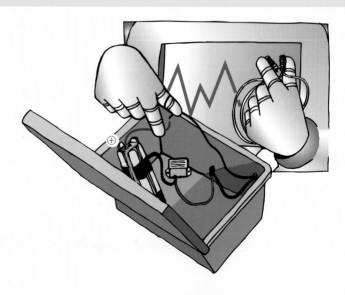

Now use those Popsicle sticks and springs!

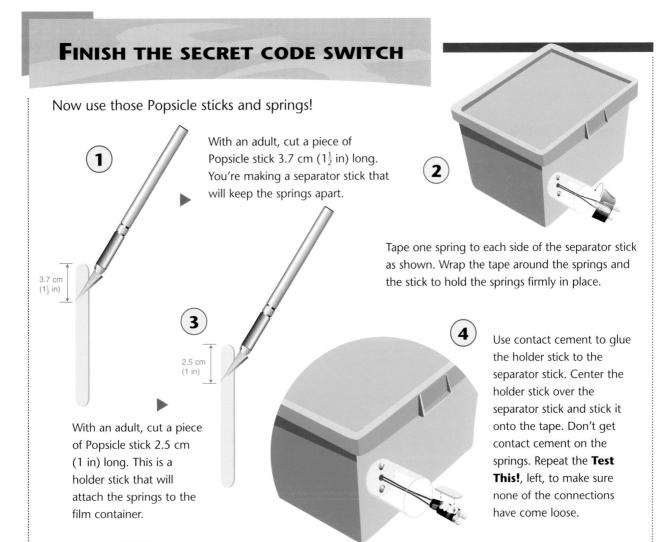

1 With an adult, cut a piece of Popsicle stick 3.7 cm (1½ in) long. You're making a separator stick that will keep the springs apart.

3.7 cm (1½ in)

2 Tape one spring to each side of the separator stick as shown. Wrap the tape around the springs and the stick to hold the springs firmly in place.

3 With an adult, cut a piece of Popsicle stick 2.5 cm (1 in) long. This is a holder stick that will attach the springs to the film container.

2.5 cm (1 in)

4 Use contact cement to glue the holder stick to the separator stick. Center the holder stick over the separator stick and stick it onto the tape. Don't get contact cement on the springs. Repeat the **Test This!**, left, to make sure none of the connections have come loose.

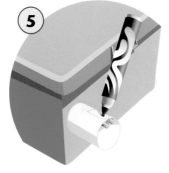

5 Go to **Troubleshoot It**, right, to put the holder stick inside the film container. Then draw a dot on the container between the springs near the lid. The dot marks the spot to dial the secret number to open the box without sounding the alarm. Go to **Test This!**, next page.

Troubleshoot It

It's tough to find the right spot to glue the holder stick inside the film container. Don't worry if you have to try it in a few places to get it exactly right. You want to put it where the springs press against the film container lid when the lid is closed. Here's what to do. Lightly tape the stick to the front edge of the container and then gently put on the lid. The lid will push the springs back to approximately the correct spot. Then move the springs slightly forward about 1 to 2 mm ($\frac{1}{32}$ to $\frac{2}{32}$ in), so they press against the lid when the lid is closed. Lightly tape the holder stick here. Now test this position by turning the lid. If the lid turns and the springs are touching, you've found the right spot. If not, try again. Once you find the right spot, mark it on the container and remove the tape from the holder stick. Then use contact cement to glue the holder stick to this spot. Whew!

Test This!

- Test the secret code switch. Close the film container lid. Turn the dial so that neither of your secret numbers is at the dot.

- Touch the unconnected wire from the film container to the wire that's connected to the ⊕ terminal of the battery pack. Listen for the bzzzzz! Way to go. It works! Skip the next step.

- If it doesn't buzz, the lid may not be pressing against the springs. To fix this, open the lid and lightly pull out the springs a bit. Now try the test again. If it still doesn't buzz, pin the springs together and listen for a buzz to check that none of the connections have come loose.

- Dial your secret number to turn the buzzer off. If it stops buzzing, the switch works. Great! Skip the next steps.

- If it doesn't stop buzzing, look inside the container and check that the springs are in place and not tangled together. The springs should never touch each other.

- Also, check that the secret numbers are well lined up with the cardboard strip and that the dot is exactly over the center between the two springs.

MAKE THE BOX TOP SWITCH

Take a bobby pin and start building a box top switch that will turn the buzzer on when the box is opened and off when the box is closed.

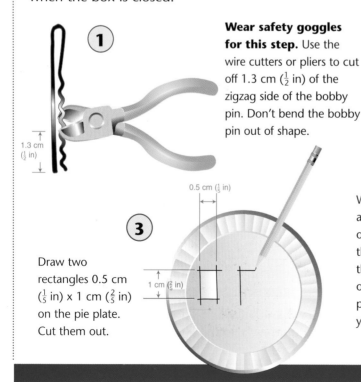

① Wear safety goggles for this step. Use the wire cutters or pliers to cut off 1.3 cm ($\frac{1}{2}$ in) of the zigzag side of the bobby pin. Don't bend the bobby pin out of shape.

1.3 cm ($\frac{1}{2}$ in)

③ Draw two rectangles 0.5 cm ($\frac{1}{5}$ in) x 1 cm ($\frac{2}{5}$ in) on the pie plate. Cut them out.

0.5 cm ($\frac{1}{5}$ in)

1 cm ($\frac{2}{5}$ in)

② Cover each end of the bobby pin with a small bit of electrical tape exactly as shown. Later, this will stop electricity from flowing through the bobby pin from one wire to another.

④ Wrap one aluminum rectangle around each of the taped ends of the bobby pin. Make sure that the aluminum covers only the tape and doesn't overlap onto the metal of the bobby pin. Trim it with the scissors if you need to.

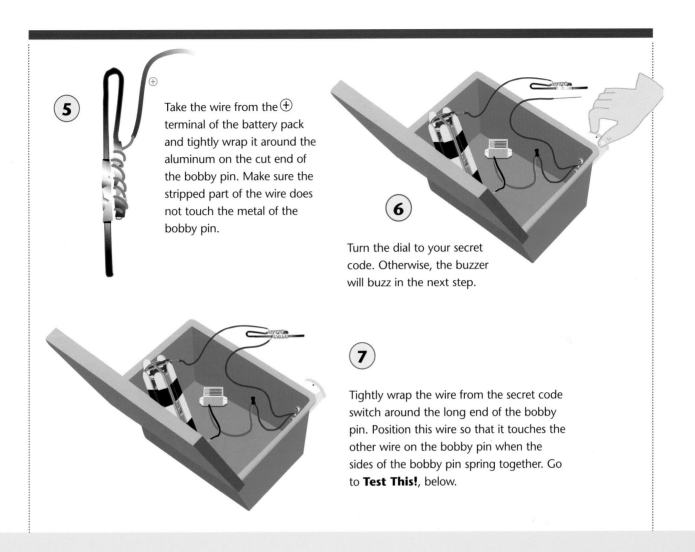

5 Take the wire from the ⊕ terminal of the battery pack and tightly wrap it around the aluminum on the cut end of the bobby pin. Make sure the stripped part of the wire does not touch the metal of the bobby pin.

6 Turn the dial to your secret code. Otherwise, the buzzer will buzz in the next step.

7 Tightly wrap the wire from the secret code switch around the long end of the bobby pin. Position this wire so that it touches the other wire on the bobby pin when the sides of the bobby pin spring together. Go to **Test This!**, below.

Test This!

- Test the box top switch. Let the two wired ends of the bobby pin spring together.
- Turn the dial so it's not on one of the secret numbers. If you hear a bzzzz, great! Gently push the bobby pin's ends apart to stop it from buzzing. Good job, you have almost completed another switch!
- If not, the wires on the bobby pin are probably not touching each other. Make sure they are firmly fastened to the aluminum and that they are on top of each other.
- Also, check that the bobby pin is not bent out of shape. You may have to bend it slightly to make the ends of the wires touch each other.

Hey, you! Test the connections you've just made.

Booby trap your box with a switch that turns on the buzzer when the box is opened.

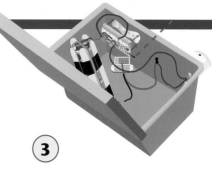

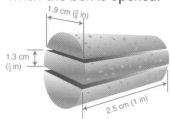

1.9 cm (³⁄₈ in)

1.3 cm (½ in)

2.5 cm (1 in)

1 On the cork, draw a rectangle as shown. Have an adult use the X-Acto knife to carefully cut it out.

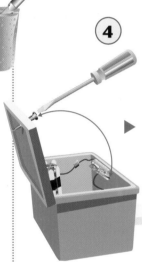

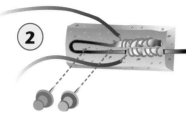

2 Attach the bobby pin to the cork. Position the bobby pin exactly as you see here. Then push the two tacks between the legs of the bobby pin.

3 Use contact cement to glue the cork inside the box. Center the long end of the bobby pin on the front panel below the top as shown.

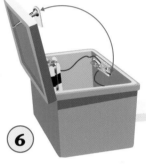

4 Use the screwdriver to screw the flat-head wood screw partway through the box lid above the long end of the bobby pin. When the lid is closed, the screw should push the bobby pin just enough to separate the ends. If it pushes too much, it will bend the bobby pin out of shape.

5

1.3 cm (½ in)

Get an adult to help you cut a piece of Popsicle stick with the X-Acto knife as shown. This piece will help push the bobby pin apart when the lid closes.

6 Glue the stick onto the screw head with contact cement as shown. Make sure the end near the front of the box lines up with the edge of the screw and the other end points toward the back of the box.

Startle Reflex

Why do alarms stop thieves in their tracks? Chances are it's because of the "startle reflex." When you hear an unexpected loud sound, your body automatically reacts beyond your control. In less than a second, your eyes blink and muscles in your face, arms, and legs tighten. It's like your muscles are trying to stop you from doing whatever you're doing, so you can deal with the cause of the noise. (Maybe the word "startled" should really be "stopled"!) Even though the startle reflex is uncontrollable, you can learn not to react if the sudden noise repeats over and over. That's why some sleepyheads end up sleeping through their wake-up alarms!

Zoom In
on the Mechanics

When you dial a secret code number, the cardboard strip, on the film canister lid in the secret code switch, comes between the two springs. Like a gate, it stops electricity, from the battery, from flowing from spring to spring to the buzzer. When you dial any other number, both springs touch the same aluminum half circle. Then electricity can flow from spring to spring to the buzzer — bzzzt! The secret code switch works with the box top switch. To make the buzzer buzz when someone opens the box, the box top switch must be on when the box is open and off when the box is closed. Here's how it works. When you close the box, the screw on the box lid pushes the wired ends of the bobby pin apart. Then electricity from the battery cannot flow from wire to wire. So the switch is off. When you open the box, the bobby pin springs together and the wires touch. Then electricity can flow, so the switch is on.

Test the Whole Kit and Caboodle

Now for the moment you've been waiting for: Use your Alarm in a Box!

- Close the box. Dial the secret code switch so it's NOT on one of your secret numbers. If it doesn't buzz, congrats — your Alarm in a Box has passed the first test! Skip the next step.
- If the buzzer buzzes when the box is closed, the box top switch isn't working well. Open the box. Then check that when the top is closed, the screw pushes the bobby pin apart, so the wired ends don't touch each other. You may have to adjust the position and length of the screw.
- Open the box top and listen for a bzzzzz!!!!!! If it buzzes, right on! Skip the next step.
- If it doesn't buzz, make sure none of the secret numbers have been dialed and that the wires on the secret code switch haven't moved. Also, check that the box top switch is working. When the top is open, the two aluminum tips of the bobby pin should touch each other. If they don't, the bobby pin may be bent. Try to fix it. Once the tips are touching, check that none of the connections have come loose.
- Close the lid. If it stops buzzing, go to the next step. If not, there's a problem somewhere. Do the checks in the step above.
- Dial your secret number to disarm the alarm. Open the box. If it doesn't buzz, your Alarm in a Box is ready for action. If it buzzes, one of the switches is not working. Recheck them.

FINISHING TOUCHES

Make sure your Alarm in a Box stays in perfect working order and dress it up to really make it your own.

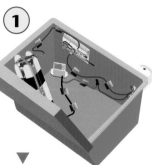

(1) ▼

Tape the buzzer and the battery pack in place as you see here. Then tape the wires to the wall, so they don't get pulled off accidentally.

(2) On the thin cardboard, trace the side wall of the box. Cut it out. ▼

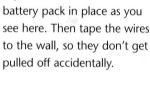

(3) Tape the cardboard cutout to the side wall to cover and protect the circuit.

(4) Decorate your box with markers, stickers, glitter, beads, shells, and the like. For safety, cover the pointy end of the screw that sticks through the lid. Then let your imagination run wild!

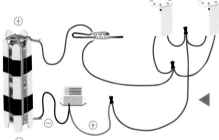

(5) ◄ You can add another number to your secret code by adding another secret code switch. For example, if your box has two secret code switches, you would need to dial two numbers, like 2 and 6, to disarm the alarm. To add more secret code switches, build them the same way and connect the switches to each other as shown.

The **Crown Jewel Capers**

Maybe the Queen of England needs an Alarm in a Box. Her crown jewels are the most costly jewelry collection in the world. Keeping them safe isn't easy:

• In 1216, King John dropped the crown jewels into quicksand.

• In 1649, Cromwell the "Lord Protector of England" chopped off the King's head and had the crown jewels smashed to bits.

• In 1661, a replacement set was made and locked up in the Tower of London.

• But in 1671, a thief tried to steal them by hitting the keeper over the head.

• In the 1700s, they were put out on display in the Jewel House, a guarded room in the Tower of London, until someone broke the state crown.

• In 1815, the Jewel House was redone so people could see the jewels but not touch.

• In 1841, a big fire broke out next door and guards had a hard time saving the jewels because no one could find the keys!

• In 1994, the jewels were put on display in a high-tech security case.

How-to Tips

DRILLING, AND CUTTING WITH X-ACTO KNIVES AND BLADES

Always have an adult help you to use a drill or to cut anything that needs an X-Acto knife or sharp blade. Don't try to cut through a bunch of thick things at once. Put some newspaper underneath the material you're cutting to protect the table or area you're cutting on.

GLUING

Try not to get glue everywhere as you use it. The step-by-step building instructions for each gadget will tell you if you need to wait for the glue to dry before you do the next step. The instructions will also tell you what type of glue to use. Regular white or brown glue works well for paper. But when you need to glue other things together, contact cement or 5-minute epoxy glue usually works better. Ask an adult for help. To use contact cement or 5-minute epoxy glue safely and correctly, follow the directions on their packages and these tips:

Cut away from your body and your hands — never cut toward them. To make a cut, put light pressure on the blade. Then pull the blade across the material. Go over the cut with the X-Acto knife until the material is cut all the way through.

• Contact Cement

Contact cement works well when the things you need to glue together have similar surfaces.

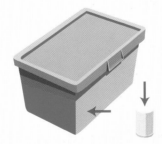

Use a Popsicle stick or toothpick to spread a thin coat of contact cement onto the surfaces you want to stick together. Be careful not to apply too much. Otherwise, the contact cement will not dry and it will become like toffee. Leave the pieces apart and let the contact cement dry for about 15 minutes.

Line up the two pieces and press them together. The contact cement will stick them together immediately and it will be completely dry in another three hours.

• Epoxy Glue

Epoxy glue is good for gluing together things that have different surfaces. You can use it to make a small pool of glue around the two surfaces. As this pool of glue dries, it will become hard like plastic.

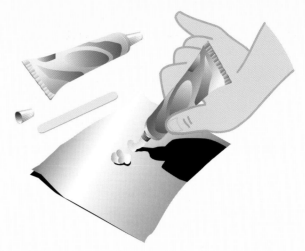

Epoxy glue usually comes in two tubes: one has sticky stuff and the other has hardener. On a piece of foil, squeeze equal small amounts out of each tube as shown. Mix them together with a Popsicle stick or toothpick.

Use a Popsicle stick or toothpick to apply the mixed epoxy glue to the two surfaces you want to stick together.

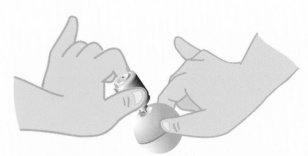

Hold the pieces together for about five minutes until the epoxy glue hardens. It will take about 24 hours for it to dry completely.

CONNECTING WIRES

To connect two wires, you need to join the metal of the wires together.

Cover the twist with electrical tape or a special plastic connector cap if you have one around. But do not use Scotch tape, masking tape, or any other non-electrical tape because the wires may heat up. Wrap electrical tape around the twist several times and cover the entire stripped part of the wire. ▼

▼

Strip about 2.5 cm (1 in) of the plastic covering from one end of each wire. See wire stripping tips, right.

Tightly twist the metal of the wires together. ▶

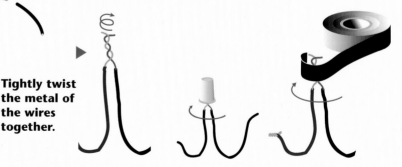

SPLITTING SPEAKER WIRES

Speaker wire is like a double wire. It is made of two wires that are attached side by side. The plastic covering on the wires joins them together, but the metal of the two wires does not touch.

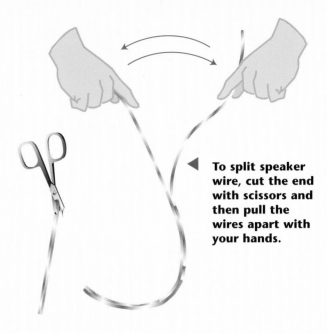

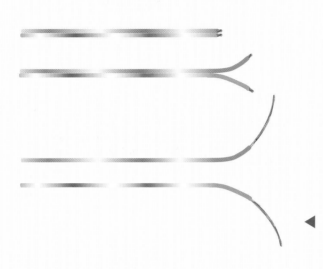

To split speaker wire, cut the end with scissors and then pull the wires apart with your hands.

In some gadgets, speaker wire is used with its two halves attached. In others, its ends are split. And in others, its two halves are split apart completely and used separately.

STRIPPING WIRES

The goal of wire stripping is to remove the plastic covering from the wire without cutting the metal of the wire. It's pretty tricky and takes lots of practice.

wire stripper

Most pliers have a wire stripper at the end of their jaws near where the handles join. If you don't have a wire stripper, you can use a nail clipper.

To strip a wire, place about 2.5 cm (1 in) of the end of it between the blades of the wire stripper or nail clippers. Lightly squeeze the handle so the blades cut only the plastic. Release the pressure a bit. Then pull the blades toward the end of the wire to remove the plastic.

The "What's That?" Glossary

archeologists: people who study human history and the history of Earth from ancient remains that are often dug up from the ground

battery: a device that changes chemical energy into electrical energy. Batteries come in many different sizes and shapes that supply different amounts of energy.

buzzer: a device that makes a buzzing sound. You may find many different types of buzzers at your local electronic store. Any one of them is fine for the gadgets in this book except for a printed-circuit (pc) mounted one. Make sure the buzzer is 3-volt DC and that it has two terminals with wires so you can connect it to a circuit. If the buzzer has two terminals but no wires, you can still use it — strip the ends of two 15 cm (6 in) long wires and connect one to each terminal. See stripping and connecting wires tips, pages 60 and 61.

chemical reaction: a change in which one or more substances form new substances by breaking down, mixing with other substances, or changing parts with other substances

circuit: a path that electric current can flow on

circuit diagram: a road map of the electrical connections needed to build a circuit like the one below. In a circuit diagram, standard symbols stand for electrical parts like wires, batteries, buzzers, and resistors. That way people who work with circuits recognize the parts right away. The lines that join parts together in a circuit diagram show that those parts are connected by a wire or by being twisted together. The length and position of these lines are not accurate. A circuit diagram shows only the connections and the order of connections.

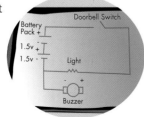

conduct: to transmit, or send, electrical energy

connection: the attachment of two or more things that conduct electricity so electricity can flow from one to the other(s)

contact: a point where two pieces of metal touch so electric current can flow from one to the other. Plastic, paper, glue, and paint can stop electricity from flowing through a contact. So be careful not to get them on contacts as you build the gadgets.

electric current: the flow of electricity

encryption: data that has been put into a secret code

enigma: something that is puzzling or cannot be explained

gauge: the thickness of a wire. The gauge number measures the diameter of the wire. For the gadgets in this book, 18 to 22 gauge wire is best. The lower the gauge number, the thicker the wire. So 18 gauge wire is thicker than 22 gauge wire.

insulation: the plastic covering on wires

key: a guide for encoding and decoding secret messages

keyword: an important word to use in an Internet search

LED: a light-emitting diode. You can find LEDs in your local electronic store or the electronic department of your local hardware store. Try to get LEDs that have long leads — 3 cm ($1\frac{1}{8}$ in). If you need lots of LEDs to make a gadget like the Secret Code Machine, for example, it will usually cost less to buy packs of LEDs rather than individual LEDs.

mechanism: a group of parts that act like a machine

motor: a machine that changes electrical energy into mechanical energy. When the motor is ON, the shaft turns.

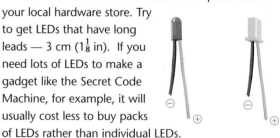

nail and screw sizes: nails and screws come in all different sizes and shapes. Here is a table that describes the dimensions for the size numbers used in this book:

Nail or Screw	Size Used in Book	Diameter in mm	Diameter in inches	Gadget	Notes
flat machine screw	4-40	2.8	7/64	Secret Code Machine, Quiz Game	-40 refers to the number of turns, but this doesn't really matter. Any number is OK. Machine screws are not pointy at the end — they're flat.
wood screw	4	2.8	7/64	Secret Code Machine, Quiz Game, Alarm in a Box	Wood screws have a pointy end. They may also be marked size 4-40, or 4-#. That is OK.
washer	4	2.8	7/64	Secret Code Machine, Quiz Game	Used with size 4 screws
washer	6	3.5	9/64	Secret Code Machine, Quiz Game	Can also be used with size 4 screws
nut	4	2.8	7/64	Secret Code Machine, Quiz Game, Alarm in a Box	Used with size 4 screws
common nail	–	–	–	Secret Code Machine, Quiz Game	Small straight nail with a flat 18 gauge

negative: see terminal

positive: see terminal

power: energy to do work

resistor: a device that cuts down the electrical power that flows through a system. The rate at which it cuts down power is measured in ohms.

speaker wire: is like a double wire. It's made of two wires that are attached side by side. Its plastic covering joins the wires together, but the metal of the two wires does not touch. Speaker wire is the recommended wire for the gadgets in this book. Although you can use other electrical wire, speaker wire costs less, and the most inexpensive kind works well for these gadgets.

switch: an electric device that turns something on or off. You can make many of the switches required for the gadgets in this book, but you will need to buy a few. You will find lots of different switches with different button styles and numbers of terminals at your local electronic store. An SPST switch, which is needed for the Bouncy Animal on page 22, is a "single pole, single throw" switch. That's just a way of saying that it has two terminals, and it switches one circuit on or off.

terminal: a place or wire on a device such as a battery, buzzer, or light bulb where an electrical connection is made or broken so the device can get or give power. Sometimes terminals and terminal wires are called contact points or connectors. They're usually marked positive ⊕ or negative ⊖ to show how they should be connected. The step-by-step instructions for building the gadgets say what to connect to the ⊕ and ⊖ terminals.

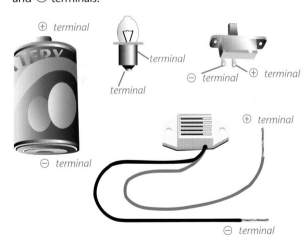

volt: the unit used to measure the amount of electricity between two terminals in a circuit

slide switch   toggle switch

terminals   terminals

Index